■ SCHOLASTIC

Extra Practice Math Centers

Addition, Subtraction & More

BY **Mary Peterson**

New York • Toronto • London • Auckland • Sydney
Mexico City • New Delhi • Hong Kong • Buenos Aires

Teaching *Resources*

Editor: Kathy Fitzgibbon
Cover design by Lillian Kohli
Cover illustration and interior illustration by Kelly Kennedy
Interior design by Holly Grundon
Interior illustrations by Eldon Doty

ISBN-13 978-0-439-76202-1
ISBN-10 0-439-76202-2

2 3 4 5 6 7 8 9 10   40   12 11 10 09 08 07

Contents

Introduction

Welcome to *Extra Practice Math Centers: Addition, Subtraction, and More*. In my classroom, I find that many students need extra practice with math skills, even though we have to keep moving through the math curriculum. I created this collection of fun and interactive story problem cards and games to engage my students and give them the extra practice they need to master important math skills. These games have been tried and tested in my classroom. Children love them, beg for them, and will play them over and over. Teachers also love them because they can see the educational benefits.

How to Use These Extra Practice Math Centers

Math Center

After a game is introduced to the group, place it in a tub at the math center. Choice is highly motivating to students. The math center can be a choice during center time, or students can choose games or puzzles from the math center when they are finished with class assignments. This is a great way to keep them busy and independent. Students love the math center so much that it can be used as a reward. For example, everyone who brings back his or her math homework may have 15 minutes of extra math center time.

Rotating Math Stations

Students absolutely enjoy math stations. Divide the class into groups, and give each group a game. You can choose games that focus on the same math skill or a variety of skills. Every 10 to 15 minutes, rotate the games to a different group or rotate the students to a different station. If it is the first time you are introducing the games, invite parents or older students to the classroom to work at each station to give students extra support. This really helps things run smoothly. Then the games can be added to the math center for choice time.

Small-Group Instruction

You can use these games to reteach a skill or to give extra help to a small group of students. The students will become so engaged playing the game with you that they won't realize they are getting remedial help. Since the games are self-explanatory, they are also useful for tutors or parent helpers working with individuals or small groups. The tutors will enjoy playing the games as much as the students.

Ten Key Educational Benefits

- Much more fun than "drill and kill"

- Significantly increases math achievement

- Instant engagement for students who say, "I'm finished, now what can I do?"

- Keeps students working independently while the teacher works with small groups

- Allows for student choice

- Gives students repeated math practice while they think they are just playing

- Supported by research on how children learn

- Gives students opportunities to work cooperatively

- Great rainy day math fun

- Inexpensive and easy to implement!

The Games: How to Make Them and Store Them

For sturdy games that will last a long time, copy the pages onto card stock and then laminate them. If you copy all the pages for one game or puzzle on the same color of card stock, it will be easier to keep track of the pieces. Plastic storage bags work well for game storage because they hold all the small pieces. Attach the directions on the outside of the storage bag with clear contact paper. Store all the games for the same math skill in a shoe box or tub so they can be easily located when you are ready to use them.

Story Problem Mats

These mats give students hands-on practice in solving story problems because they help students visualize how to solve a problem. Students can work in small groups or independently using the manipulatives to solve math problems. Store each story problem mat in a separate one-gallon-size plastic storage bag or a tub with the suggested manipulatives. I also suggest that you laminate each story problem mat.

Board Games

The board games are very simple to play and a favorite of students. Players solve a math problem and then move around the board to be the first one to the end of the path. Most of the games have an answer key for self-checking. The board games are on two pages. They can be laminated separately and then taped together. When the game boards are folded in half, they will fit in a one-gallon-size plastic storage bag. Tape the directions for the game on the outside of the storage bag. The game cards have a picture or words on the face to identify them. Keep everything needed to play the game in the same storage bag. Some good place markers for the games include different shapes and colors of erasers, plastic toys, pencil toppers, chess pieces, and leftover game pieces from old board games. Some games have spinners. A fast and easy way to make a spinner is to fasten a paper clip to the center of the spinner with a brass fastener. You can also purchase metal spinners at teacher supply stores.

Card Games

The card games are simple yet fun to play and are modeled after many of the old favorites. Using a different color of card stock for each game will help you keep the games separate. Identifying words or pictures appear on the face of each card. Cut apart the cards and keep them and all other materials needed for one game in a one-quart-size plastic storage bag. Attach the game directions to the front of the storage bag.

Puzzles

The puzzles can be pieced together independently or with a partner. Students enjoy being able to self-check their answers by seeing if the puzzle is put together correctly. When copying the puzzles, make sure to copy the picture on the back of the answer page. Copy each puzzle on a different color of card stock, as these pieces can get mixed up easily. Cut apart the cards with the picture on the back. Students read the math problem on the game board and cover it with the correct answer card. Then they flip over the answer cards. If the answers are correct, the picture puzzle has been put together correctly. Keep each game board and accompanying puzzle pieces in a separate plastic storage bag. Attach the directions and a small picture of the completed puzzle on the outside.

Addition and Subtraction Centers

Story Problem Cards and Mats

....

Board Games

....

Puzzles

....

Story Problem Cards and Mats

Directions:

1. Laminate the story problem cards. Write numbers on the blank lines with an erasable marker so you can change the numbers.

2. Give the manipulatives listed below to students so they can solve the problems on the story cards. After students solve the problem on the card, have them write and illustrate the problems in their math journals.

Bird Nests (page 8)
Students place the eggs in each bird's nest. Then they subtract to find out how many more eggs Brenda Bird has.

Manipulatives: dried white beans, egg-shaped erasers, or jelly beans

Barnyard (pages 9–10)
Students cut out the animals on page 10 and put them in the barnyard. Then they count all the animals.

Crayon Boxes (page 11)
Students place crayons in each box and then add them all together.

Manipulatives: crayons

Shell Bucket (page 12)
Students put shells in the bucket. Then they add more shells. They count how many shells they have in all.
Manipulatives: small shells

School Bus (page 13)
Students place children on the buses. They count how many children are on all the buses.

Manipulatives: smiley face erasers or dried lima beans with faces drawn on them

Cookie Jar (page 14)
Students put cookies in the jar and then take some away. They count how many cookies are left in the jar.

Manipulatives: animal crackers or mini-size cookies

Piggy Bank (page 15)
Students place pennies in each piggy bank. They subtract to find out how many fewer pennies José has.

Manipulatives: real or plastic pennies

Apple Tree (page 16)
Students put apples on the tree. They pick some and place them in the basket. They count how many apples are left on the tree.

Manipulatives: apple erasers or dried beans painted red and green

Clowns (page 17)
Students place balls on the clowns like they are juggling. They subtract to find the difference in the number of balls the clowns can juggle.

Manipulatives: small pom-poms or dried beans

Sally Bird has _____ eggs in her nest.

Brenda Bird has _____ eggs in her nest.

How many more eggs does Brenda Bird have?

Sally Bird

Brenda Bird

There are _____ cows, _____ sheep,

_____ pigs, and _____ horses in the

barnyard. What is the sum of all the animals

in the barnyard?

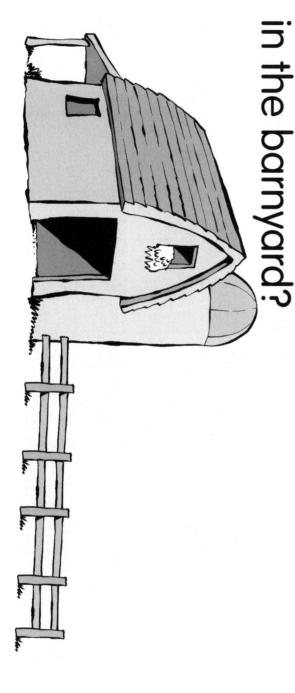

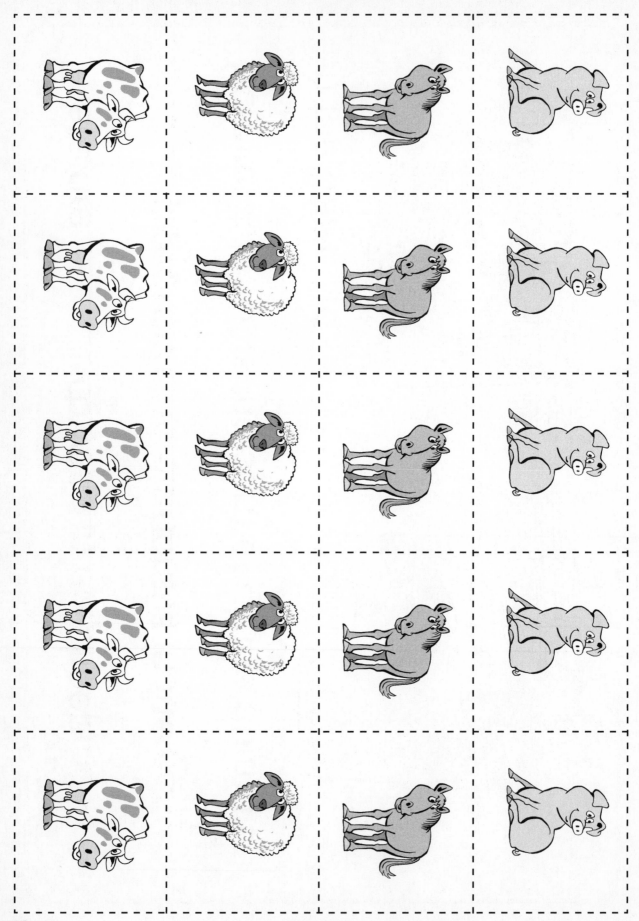

There are _____ crayons in one box and _____ crayons in the other box. How many crayons are in both boxes?

Jacob is finding shells on the beach.

He has _____ shells in his bucket.

If he finds _____ more

shells, how many

shells will he

have in all?

 Extra Practice Math Centers: Addition, Subtraction, & More © 2007 by Mary Peterson, Scholastic Teaching Resources

There are _____ children on bus A,

_____ children on bus B, and

_____ children on bus C. All together,

how many children are on the buses?

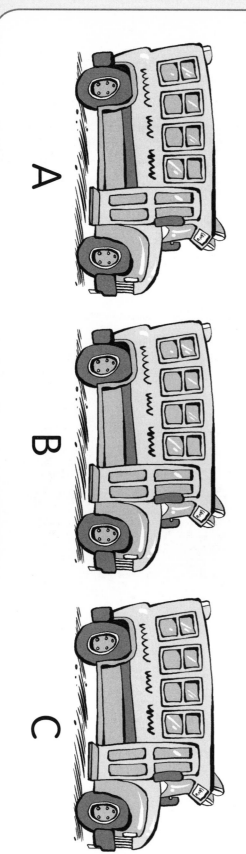

A   B   C

There are _____ cookies in the cookie jar. If Matthew takes _____ cookies, how many cookies will be left in the cookie jar?

Extra Practice Math Centers: Addition, Subtraction, & More © 2007 by Mary Peterson, Scholastic Teaching Resources

Elena has ———— pennies in her piggy bank.

José has ———— pennies in his piggy bank.

How many fewer pennies does José have?

Elena's
bank

José's
bank

Extra Practice Math Centers: Addition, Subtraction, & More © 2007 by Mary Peterson, Scholastic Teaching Resources

There are _____ apples on the tree.

Hannah picks _____ apples and puts

them in a basket.

How many apples are _____

left on the tree?

One clown can juggle _____ balls at a time.

The other clown can juggle _____ balls.

What is the difference in the number of balls they can juggle?

Bean Pot Math

Directions:

Manipulatives: dried beans

1. Place a handful of beans on the pot. Players place their markers in the Start space.

2. Players take turns spinning and moving markers around the board. When a player lands on a number, he or she removes that number of real beans from the pot and keeps them.

3. When a player lands on a Bean Card space, he or she draws a card and says the number of beans on the card. Then the player adds enough of his or her real beans to the number of beans on the card to form a group of ten. For example, if a card shows six beans, a player adds four real beans to make ten beans. Play continues until all beans are gone from the pot. The player with the greatest number of tens wins.

 Extra Practice Math Centers: Addition, Subtraction, & More © 2007 by Mary Peterson, Scholastic Teaching Resources

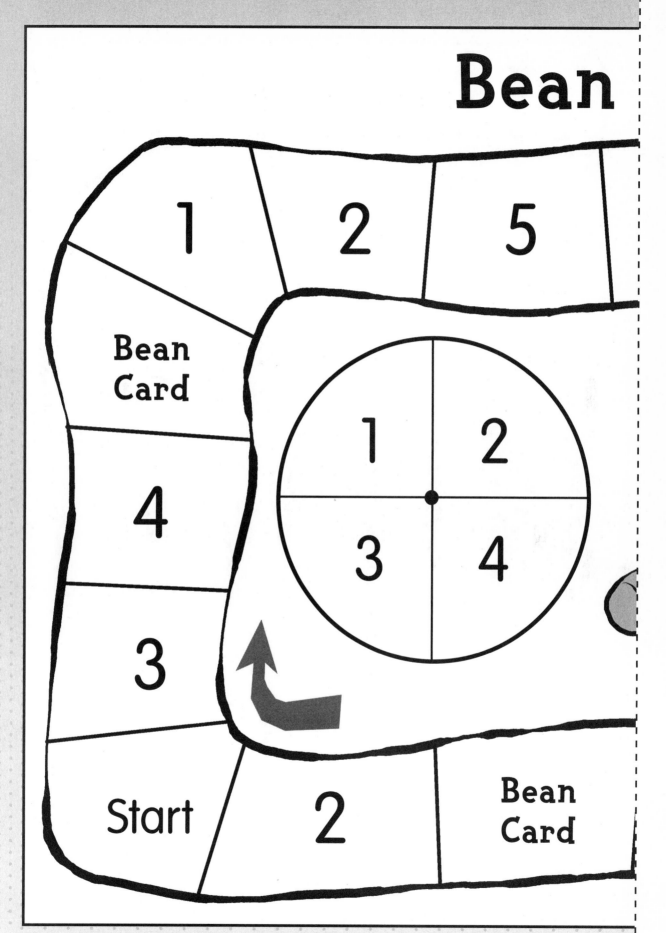

Pot Math

Bean Pot Math Game Card

Bean Pot Math Game Card

Bean Pot Math Game Card

Bean Pot Math Game Card

Bean Pot Math Game Card

Bean Pot Math Game Card

Bean Pot Math Game Card

Bean Pot Math Game Card

Bean Pot Math Game Card

Bean Pot Math Game Card

Bean Pot Math Game Card

Bean Pot Math Game Card

Bean Pot Math Game Card

Bean Pot Math Game Card

Bean Pot Math Game Card

Bean Pot Math Game Card

Bean Pot Math Game Card

Bean Pot Math Game Card

Extra Practice Math Centers: Addition, Subtraction, & More © 2007 by Mary Peterson, Scholastic Teaching Resources

**Bean Pot Math
Game Card**

**Bean Pot Math
Game Card**

**Bean Pot Math
Game Card**

**Bean Pot Math
Game Card**

**Bean Pot Math
Game Card**

**Bean Pot Math
Game Card**

**Bean Pot Math
Game Card**

**Bean Pot Math
Game Card**

**Bean Pot Math
Game Card**

Addition Spin and Search

Directions:

1. The first player spins both spinners and adds the two numbers together.

2. The player then searches the game board to find the shape with the answer. He or she takes the matching shape card. For each turn, a player solves only one addition problem.

3. Players may collect only one of each shape card. If a player cannot take a shape card, the next player takes a turn. The first player to collect all eight shape cards is the winner.

Addition Spin and Search
Game Board

Extra Practice Math Centers: Addition, Subtraction, & More © 2007 by Mary Peterson, Scholastic Teaching Resources

Addition Spin and Search
Game Board

12   20

5   17

14

9   11

16

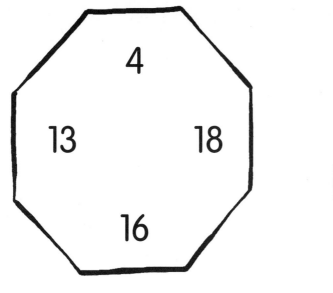

4

13   18

16

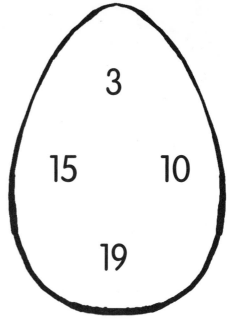

3

15   10

19

Addition Spin and Search Game Cards

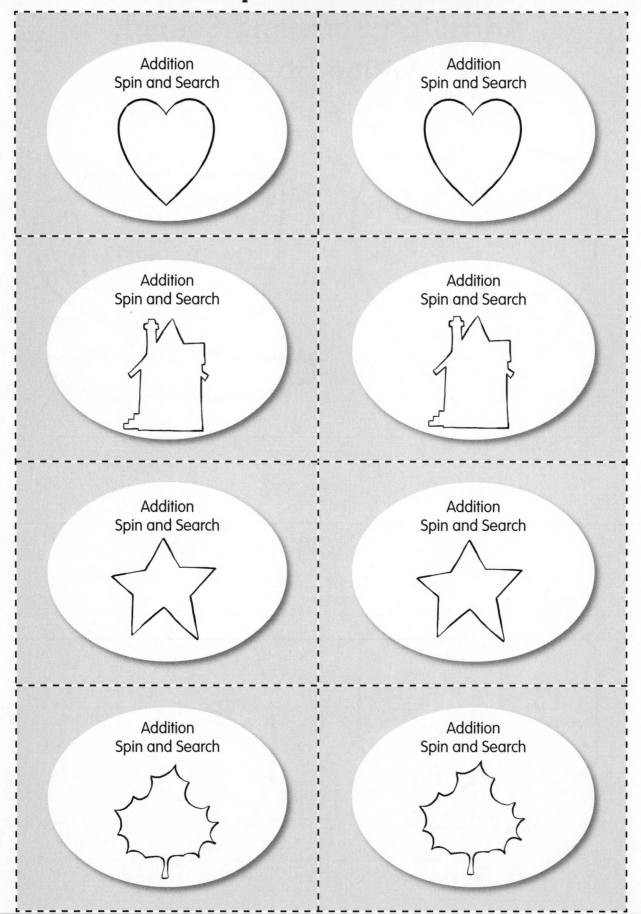

Extra Practice Math Centers: Addition, Subtraction, & More © 2007 by Mary Peterson, Scholastic Teaching Resources

Addition
Spin and Search

Addition
Spin and Search

Addition
Spin and Search

Addition
Spin and Search

Addition
Spin and Search

Addition
Spin and Search

Addition
Spin and Search

Addition
Spin and Search

Rainy Day Math

Directions:

1. Players place their markers on the Start space. The first player draws a problem card. He or she reads the card, decides whether to add or subtract, and solves the problem. Another player uses the answer card to check the answer. If the answer is correct, the first player moves the number of spaces indicated on the problem card.

2. Each player, in turn, draws a card, solves the problem, and moves if the answer is correct. The first player to reach the house is the winner.

Answer Card

1. 5 buttons	**11.** 15 fish
2. 15 ducks	**12.** 7 fish
3. 4 ladybugs	**13.** 16 children
4. 9 books	**14.** 16 minutes
5. 12 gumballs	**15.** 2 caterpillars
6. 5 minutes	**16.** 14 butterflies
7. 19 cents	**17.** 3 apples
8. 4 pennies	**18.** 15 tacos
9. 7 white cars	**19.** 8 rocks
10. 7 tomatoes	**20.** 8 pennies

Extra Practice Math Centers: Addition, Subtraction, & More © 2007 by Mary Peterson, Scholastic Teaching Resources

Rainy Day

Start

You forgot to button your coat. Lose 1 turn.

It's a downpour! Go back 2 spaces.

Stop to look at a rainbow. Lose 1 turn.

Math

You forgot your book. Go back to Start.

It stopped raining. Go ahead 2 spaces.

You fell in a puddle. Lose 1 turn.

Finish

It's another downpour! Go back 2 spaces.

Hurray! You made it home!

Rainy Day Math

1. There are 8 buttons on a coat. 3 fell off. How many buttons are left?
Move 2 spaces

Rainy Day Math

2. 7 ducks are swimming in the pond. 8 more ducks join them. How many ducks are there in all?
Move 3 spaces

Rainy Day Math

3. 10 ladybugs are on the flower. 6 flew away. How many ladybugs are left on the flower? **Move 1 space**

Rainy Day Math

4. Andrew got 4 books from the library. His mom gave him 5 more books. How many books does Andrew have in all? **Move 2 spaces**

Rainy Day Math

5. Li has 3 gumballs, Darren has 5 gumballs, and Alberto has 4 gumballs. How many gumballs do they have altogether? **Move 3 spaces**

Rainy Day Math

6. Mia finished her math in 10 minutes. Joey took 15 minutes to finish. How many more minutes did it take Joey to finish? **Move 1 space**

Rainy Day Math

7. Lucy spent 8 cents on candy and 11 cents on a cupcake. What is the total amount Lucy spent?
Move 2 spaces

Rainy Day Math

8. Emily bought gum for 6 cents. She gave the clerk a dime. How many pennies will Emily get in change?
Move 3 spaces

Rainy Day Math

9. Tom has 15 toy cars in his collection. 8 are black and the rest are white. How many cars are white?
Move 1 space

Rainy Day Math

10. Jayden picked 18 tomatoes in the garden. She sold 11 of them. How many tomatoes does Jayden have left? **Move 2 spaces**

Rainy Day Math

11. Carl caught 9 fish. His dad caught 6 fish. How many fish did they catch altogether?
Move 2 spaces

Rainy Day Math

12. Kayla caught 9 fish. Her dad caught 16 fish. How many more fish did Dad catch than Kayla?
Move 3 spaces

Rainy Day Math

13. There are 9 children in the toy store. 7 more children come in. How many children are in the toy store?
Move 1 space

Rainy Day Math

14. Jill read a book for 11 minutes this morning and 5 minutes this afternoon. How long did Jill read her book today? **Move 2 spaces**

Rainy Day Math

15. Taylor found 6 caterpillars. Justin found 8 caterpillars. How many more caterpillars did Justin find?
Move 3 spaces

Rainy Day Math

16. Selena saw 6 butterflies. Ian saw 8 butterflies. How many butterflies did they see altogether?
Move 1 space

Rainy Day Math

17. Ben picked 9 apples. Alice picked 6 apples. What is the difference in the number of apples they picked?
Move 2 spaces

Rainy Day Math

18. Robert made 9 tacos. Megan made 6 tacos. What is the total number of tacos they made?
Move 3 spaces

Rainy Day Math

19. Marc has 18 rocks in his collection. He bought 10 at the store. He found the rest. How many rocks did Marc find? **Move 1 space**

Rainy Day Math

20. Jessie bought candy for 12 cents. He gave the clerk 20 cents. How many pennies will he get back in change? **Move 2 spaces**

Alligator Subtraction

Directions:

1. Players place their markers on the mother alligator. The first player draws a card, solves the subtraction problem, and checks the answer against the answer card. If the answer is correct, the player moves the marker to the space with that answer. If the answer is incorrect, the player stays put.

2. The first player to get to the baby alligator is the winner.

Answer Card				
6 – 5 = 1	7 – 5 = 2	7 – 6 = 1	8 – 5 = 3	8 – 6 = 2
8 – 7 = 1	9 – 5 = 4	9 – 6 = 3	9 – 7 = 2	9 – 8 = 1
10 – 5 = 5	10 – 6 = 4	10 – 7 = 3	10 – 8 = 2	10 – 9 = 1
11 – 5 = 6	11 – 6 = 5	11 – 7 = 4	11 – 8 = 3	11 – 9 = 2
12 – 5 = 7	12 – 6 = 6	12 – 7 = 5	12 – 8 = 4	12 – 9 = 3
13 – 5 = 8	13 – 6 = 7	13 – 7 = 6	13 – 8 = 5	13 – 9 = 4
14 – 5 = 9	14 – 6 = 8	14 – 7 = 7	14 – 8 = 6	14 – 9 = 5
15 – 6 = 9	15 – 7 = 8	15 – 8 = 7	15 – 9 = 6	16 – 7 = 9
16 – 8 = 8	16 – 9 = 7	17 – 8 = 9	17 – 9 = 8	18 – 9 = 9

Alligator

Start

Subtraction

Finish

Alligator Subtraction
11 – 8

Alligator Subtraction
10 – 8

Alligator Subtraction
9 – 8

Alligator Subtraction
16 – 7

Alligator Subtraction
15 – 7

Alligator Subtraction
14 – 7

Alligator Subtraction
13 – 7

Alligator Subtraction
12 – 7

Alligator Subtraction
11 – 7

Alligator Subtraction
10 – 7

Alligator Subtraction
9 – 7

Alligator Subtraction
8 – 7

Alligator Subtraction
15 – 6

Alligator Subtraction
14 – 6

Alligator Subtraction
13 – 6

Alligator Subtraction

$12 - 6$

Alligator Subtraction

$11 - 6$

Alligator Subtraction

$10 - 6$

Alligator Subtraction

$9 - 6$

Alligator Subtraction

$8 - 6$

Alligator Subtraction

$7 - 6$

Alligator Subtraction

$14 - 5$

Alligator Subtraction

$13 - 5$

Alligator Subtraction

$12 - 5$

Alligator Subtraction

$11 - 5$

Alligator Subtraction

$10 - 5$

Alligator Subtraction

$9 - 5$

Alligator Subtraction

$8 - 5$

Alligator Subtraction

$7 - 5$

Alligator Subtraction

$6 - 5$

Alligator Subtraction
18 – 9

Alligator Subtraction
17 – 9

Alligator Subtraction
16 – 9

Alligator Subtraction
15 – 9

Alligator Subtraction
14 – 9

Alligator Subtraction
13 – 9

Alligator Subtraction
12 – 9

Alligator Subtraction
11 – 9

Alligator Subtraction
10 – 9

Alligator Subtraction
17 – 8

Alligator Subtraction
16 – 8

Alligator Subtraction
15 – 8

Alligator Subtraction
14 – 8

Alligator Subtraction
13 – 8

Alligator Subtraction
12 – 8

Fact Family

Directions:

1. Players place their markers on the Start space. The first player draws a house card and figures out by adding or subtracting which fact family member is missing. If the answer is correct, the player spins the spinner and moves that number of spaces. If the answer is incorrect, his or her turn ends.

2. The first player to get to the house is the winner.

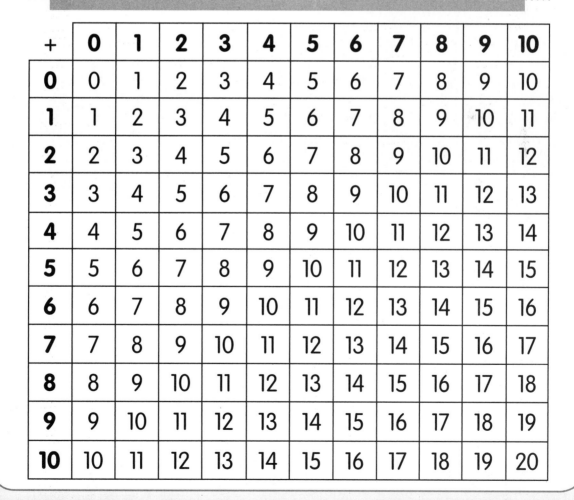

+	0	1	2	3	4	5	6	7	8	9	10
0	0	1	2	3	4	5	6	7	8	9	10
1	1	2	3	4	5	6	7	8	9	10	11
2	2	3	4	5	6	7	8	9	10	11	12
3	3	4	5	6	7	8	9	10	11	12	13
4	4	5	6	7	8	9	10	11	12	13	14
5	5	6	7	8	9	10	11	12	13	14	15
6	6	7	8	9	10	11	12	13	14	15	16
7	7	8	9	10	11	12	13	14	15	16	17
8	8	9	10	11	12	13	14	15	16	17	18
9	9	10	11	12	13	14	15	16	17	18	19
10	10	11	12	13	14	15	16	17	18	19	20

Fact Family

Start

Go ahead 3.

Go back to Start.

Go back 3.

Go back to Start.

Go ahead 3.

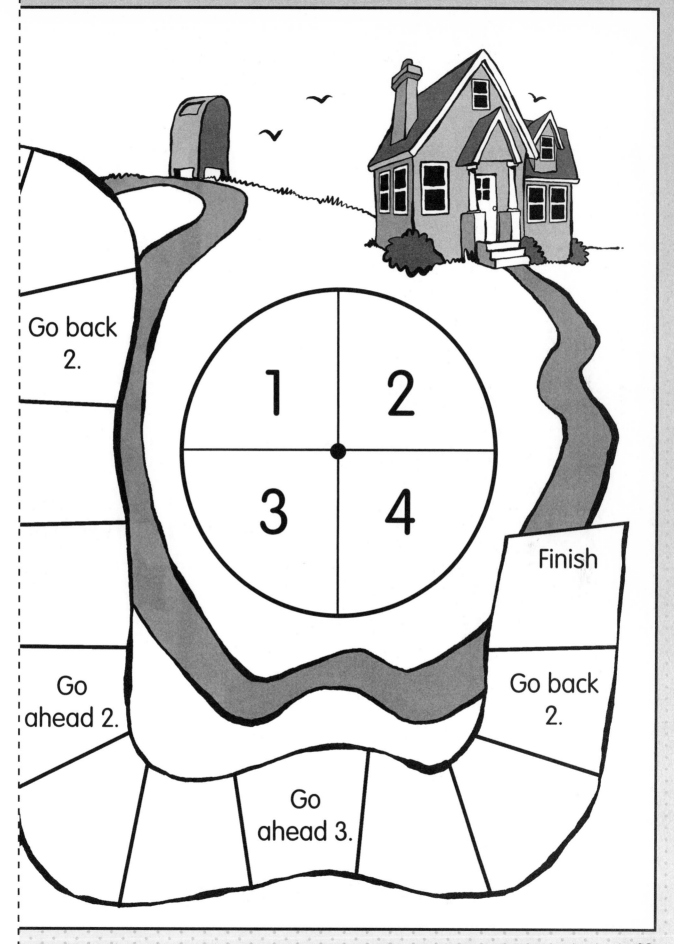

Go back 2.

1 2
3 4

Go ahead 2.

Finish

Go back 2.

Go ahead 3.

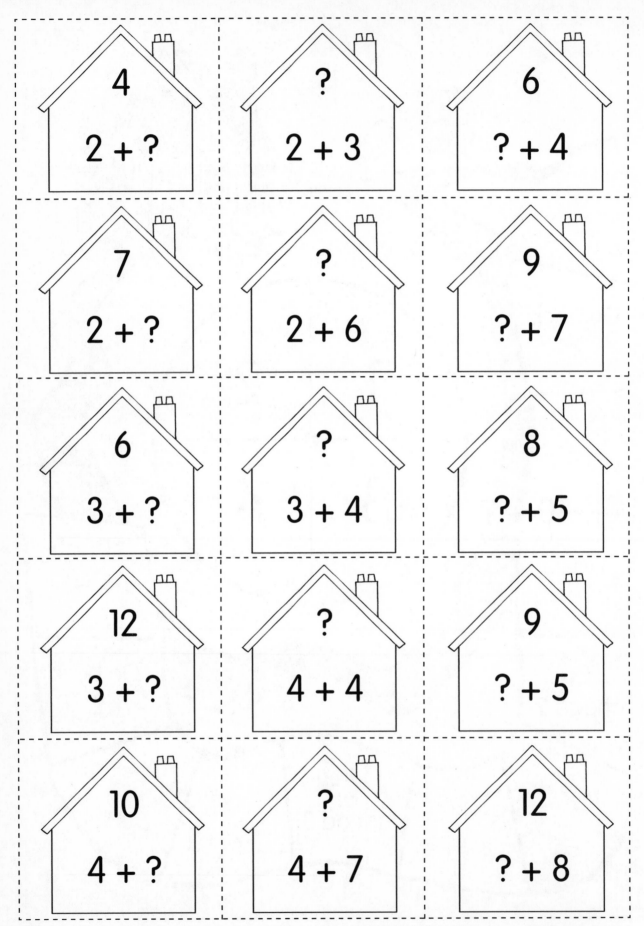

4
2 + ?

?
2 + 3

6
? + 4

7
2 + ?

?
2 + 6

9
? + 7

6
3 + ?

?
3 + 4

8
? + 5

12
3 + ?

?
4 + 4

9
? + 5

10
4 + ?

?
4 + 7

12
? + 8

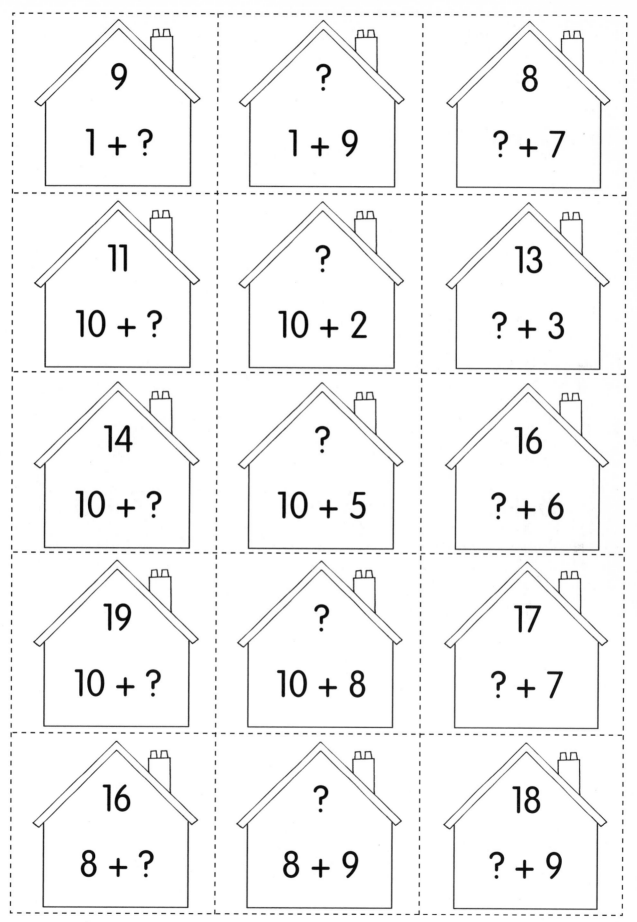

9 1 + ?	? 1 + 9	8 ? + 7
11 10 + ?	? 10 + 2	13 ? + 3
14 10 + ?	? 10 + 5	16 ? + 6
19 10 + ?	? 10 + 8	17 ? + 7
16 8 + ?	? 8 + 9	18 ? + 9

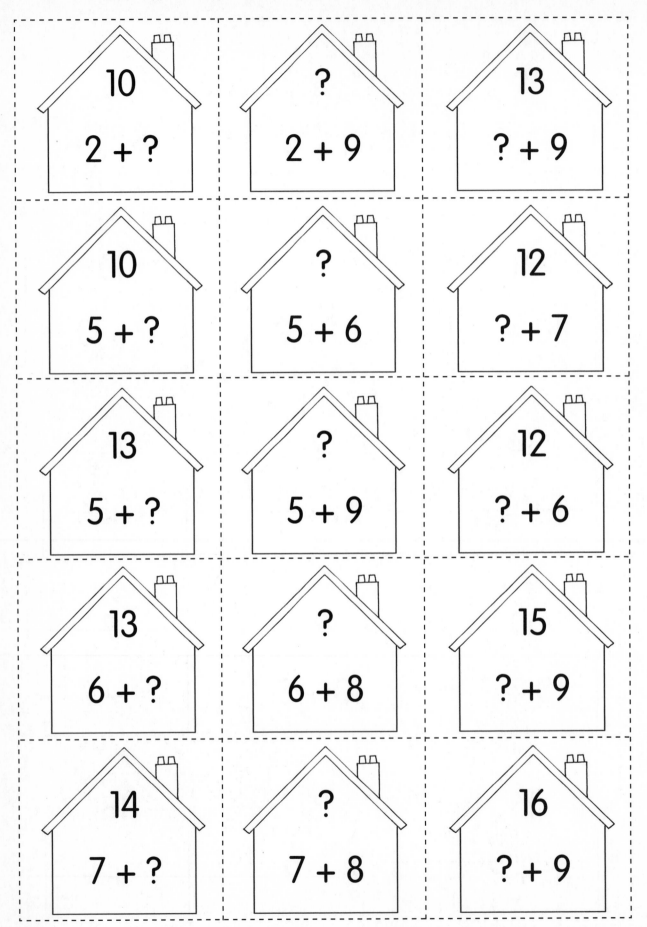

10
2 + ?

?
2 + 9

13
? + 9

10
5 + ?

?
5 + 6

12
? + 7

13
5 + ?

?
5 + 9

12
? + 6

13
6 + ?

?
6 + 8

15
? + 9

14
7 + ?

?
7 + 8

16
? + 9

 Extra Practice Math Centers: Addition, Subtraction, & More © 2007 by Mary Peterson, Scholastic Teaching Resources

Addition Puzzles

Directions:

1. For each puzzle, make a two-sided copy with the picture puzzle on one side and the answer cards on the other side. Cut apart the answer cards. (Note: Copy each puzzle onto different colors of card stock.)

2. The page that shows the corresponding addition expressions is the game board.

3. Students read an addition expression on the game board. Then they cover it with the correct answer card.

4. When answer cards cover the entire game board, students turn over the cards. If the picture puzzle is put together correctly, all the sums are correct. If the puzzle is not put together correctly, have students check their sums.

Addition Puzzle 1 Game Board

Addition Puzzle 1 7 + 9	Addition Puzzle 1 9 + 9	Addition Puzzle 1 2 + 3
Addition Puzzle 1 3 + 3	Addition Puzzle 1 5 + 6	Addition Puzzle 1 6 + 6
Addition Puzzle 1 4 + 4	Addition Puzzle 1 7 + 8	Addition Puzzle 1 4 + 5
Addition Puzzle 1 5 + 5	Addition Puzzle 1 8 + 9	Addition Puzzle 1 6 + 7
Addition Puzzle 1 7 + 7	Addition Puzzle 1 10 + 10	Addition Puzzle 1 3 + 4

Addition Puzzle 1 Answer Cards

Addition
Puzzle 1

5

Addition
Puzzle 1

18

Addition
Puzzle 1

16

Addition
Puzzle 1

12

Addition
Puzzle 1

11

Addition
Puzzle 1

6

Addition
Puzzle 1

9

Addition
Puzzle 1

15

Addition
Puzzle 1

8

Addition
Puzzle 1

13

Addition
Puzzle 1

17

Addition
Puzzle 1

10

Addition
Puzzle 1

7

Addition
Puzzle 1

20

Addition
Puzzle 1

14

Extra Practice Math Centers: Addition, Subtraction, & More © 2007 by Mary Peterson, Scholastic Teaching Resources

Addition Puzzle 2 Game Board

Addition Puzzle 2 **8 + 8**	Addition Puzzle 2 **10 + 8**	Addition Puzzle 2 **1 + 4**
Addition Puzzle 2 **2 + 4**	Addition Puzzle 2 **7 + 4**	Addition Puzzle 2 **4 + 8**
Addition Puzzle 2 **3 + 5**	Addition Puzzle 2 **6 + 9**	Addition Puzzle 2 **3 + 6**
Addition Puzzle 2 **4 + 6**	Addition Puzzle 2 **6 + 11**	Addition Puzzle 2 **5 + 8**
Addition Puzzle 2 **4 + 10**	Addition Puzzle 2 **9 + 11**	Addition Puzzle 2 **2 + 5**

Addition Puzzle 2 Answer Cards

Addition Puzzle 2

5

Addition Puzzle 2

18

Addition Puzzle 2

16

Addition Puzzle 2

12

Addition Puzzle 2

11

Addition Puzzle 2

6

Addition Puzzle 2

9

Addition Puzzle 2

15

Addition Puzzle 2

8

Addition Puzzle 2

13

Addition Puzzle 2

17

Addition Puzzle 2

10

Addition Puzzle 2

7

Addition Puzzle 2

20

Addition Puzzle 2

14

Place Value Centers

Story Problem Cards and Mats

Board Games

Card Games

Puzzles

Extra Practice Math Centers: Addition, Subtraction, & More © 2007 by Mary Peterson, Scholastic Teaching Resources

Number Muncher

Directions:

1. Players place their markers on Start. The first player draws a card and decides if the first number is greater than (>), less than (<), or equal to (=) the second number.

2. The second player checks the answer on the Answer Card. If the answer is correct, the player moves to the first correct sign that appears on the game board. If the answer is incorrect, the player stays put. The first player to reach the worm wins.

Answer Card					
1. >	2. =	3. <	4. >	5. =	6. <
7. <	8. >	9. <	10. <	11. <	12. <
13. >	14. =	15. >	16. <	17. =	18. <
19. >	20. <	21. >	22. >	23. =	24. <
25. <	26. >	27. =	28. =	29. >	30. =

Number Muncher

Start

Extra Practice Math Centers: Addition, Subtraction, & More © 2007 by Mary Peterson, Scholastic Teaching Resources

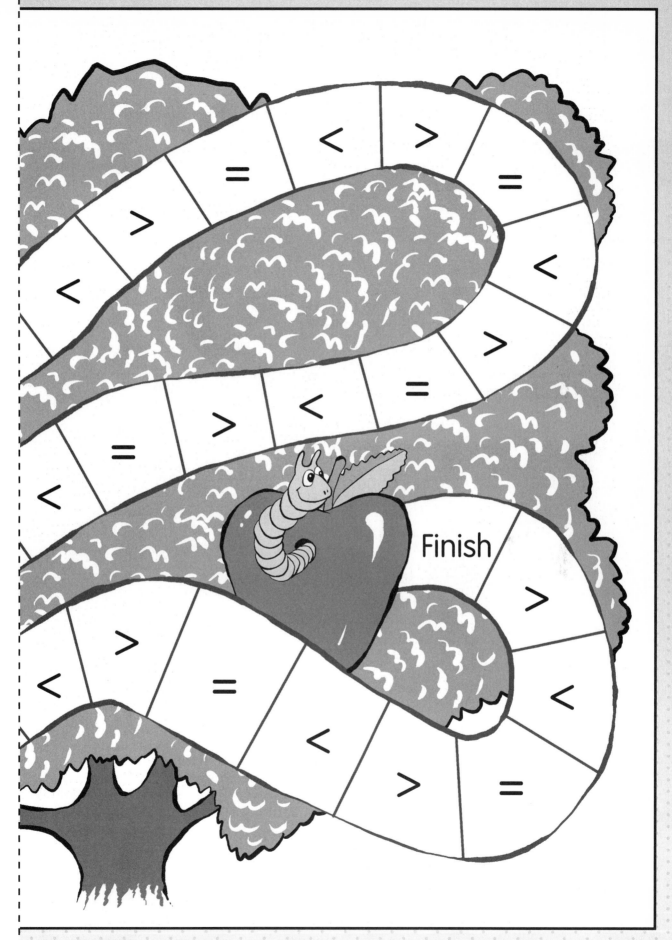

Finish

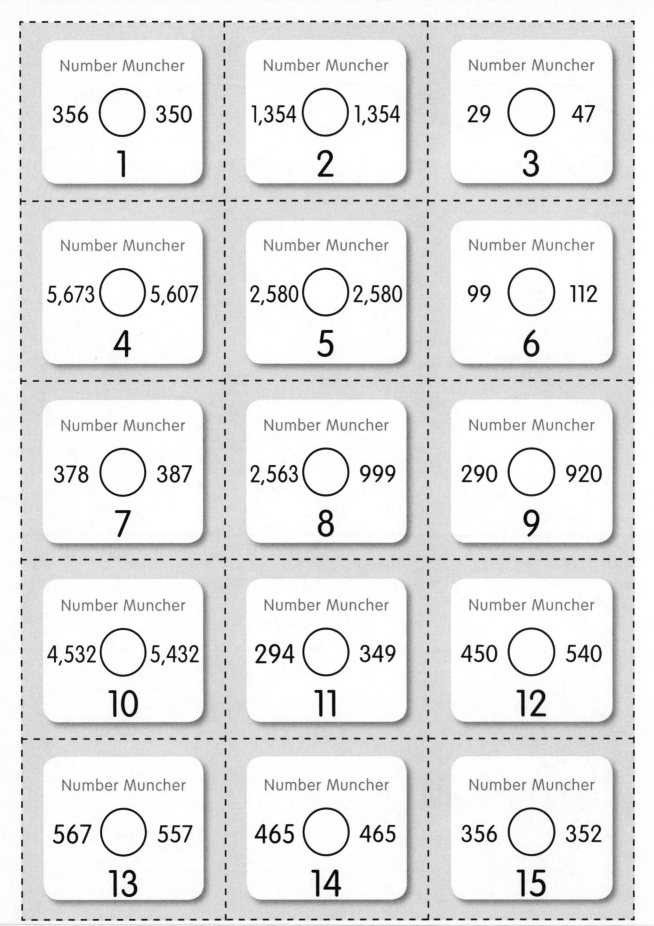

Number Muncher

356 ◯ 350

1

Number Muncher

1,354 ◯ 1,354

2

Number Muncher

29 ◯ 47

3

Number Muncher

5,673 ◯ 5,607

4

Number Muncher

2,580 ◯ 2,580

5

Number Muncher

99 ◯ 112

6

Number Muncher

378 ◯ 387

7

Number Muncher

2,563 ◯ 999

8

Number Muncher

290 ◯ 920

9

Number Muncher

4,532 ◯ 5,432

10

Number Muncher

294 ◯ 349

11

Number Muncher

450 ◯ 540

12

Number Muncher

567 ◯ 557

13

Number Muncher

465 ◯ 465

14

Number Muncher

356 ◯ 352

15

 Extra Practice Math Centers: Addition, Subtraction, & More © 2007 by Mary Peterson, Scholastic Teaching Resources

Number Muncher	Number Muncher	Number Muncher
79 ◯ 97	1,203 ◯ 1,203	209 ◯ 290
16	**17**	**18**
Number Muncher	Number Muncher	Number Muncher
4,276 ◯ 4,272	1,000 ◯ 1,100	876 ◯ 768
19	**20**	**21**
Number Muncher	Number Muncher	Number Muncher
4,021 ◯ 421	6,540 ◯ 6,540	340 ◯ 341
22	**23**	**24**
Number Muncher	Number Muncher	Number Muncher
5,699 ◯ 5,966	89 ◯ 78	784 ◯ 784
25	**26**	**27**
Number Muncher	Number Muncher	Number Muncher
9,478 ◯ 9,478	2,358 ◯ 839	5,478 ◯ 5,478
28	**29**	**30**

Get Close

Directions:

1. Shuffle and place the game cards facedown in a pile.

2. The first player draws three cards from the top of the deck and places them randomly in the hundreds, tens, and ones place on the Get Close Target Card.

3. The first player then deals six cards to each player. The players use their cards to make one three-digit number that is as close as possible to the number on the Target Card.

4. Players, in turn, reveal the numbers they formed and figure the difference between their number and the target number. The player with the lowest score is the winner.

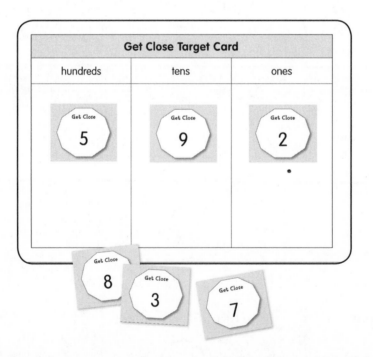

Extra Practice Math Centers: Addition, Subtraction, & More © 2007 by Mary Peterson, Scholastic Teaching Resources

Get Close Target Card

hundreds	tens	ones

Get Close

0

Get Close

1

Get Close

2

Get Close

3

Get Close

4

Get Close

5

Get Close

6

Get Close

7

Get Close

8

Get Close

9

Get Close

0

Get Close

1

Get Close

2

Get Close

3

Get Close

4

Get Close

5

Get Close

6

Get Close

7

Get Close

8

Get Close

9

Get Close

0

Get Close

1

Get Close

2

Get Close

3

Get Close

4

Get Close

5

Get Close

6

Get Close

7

Get Close

8

Get Close

9

Get Close

0

Get Close

1

Get Close

2

Get Close

3

Get Close

4

Get Close

5

Get Close

6

Get Close

7

Get Close

8

Get Close

9

Extra Practice Math Centers: Addition, Subtraction, & More © 2007 by Mary Peterson, Scholastic Teaching Resources

Place Value Picnic

Directions:

Manipulatives: a tub of base ten blocks

1. Players place their markers on the Start space. The first player draws a card and reads the number aloud.* The other players determine whether the player read the number correctly or not. If correct, the player moves the number of spaces directed on the card. The player then takes the number of base ten blocks as indicated on the game board.

2. When a player lands on Trade, all players trade in their base ten blocks (ten ones for a ten, ten tens for a hundred, and so on).

3. When a player reaches the picnic basket, all players count their base ten blocks. The player with the highest number wins.

   * For a more challenging game, another player reads the number aloud and the player must write it down correctly before they can move.

Start

Place Value Picnic

Finish

 Extra Practice Math Centers: Addition, Subtraction, & More © 2007 by Mary Peterson, Scholastic Teaching Resources

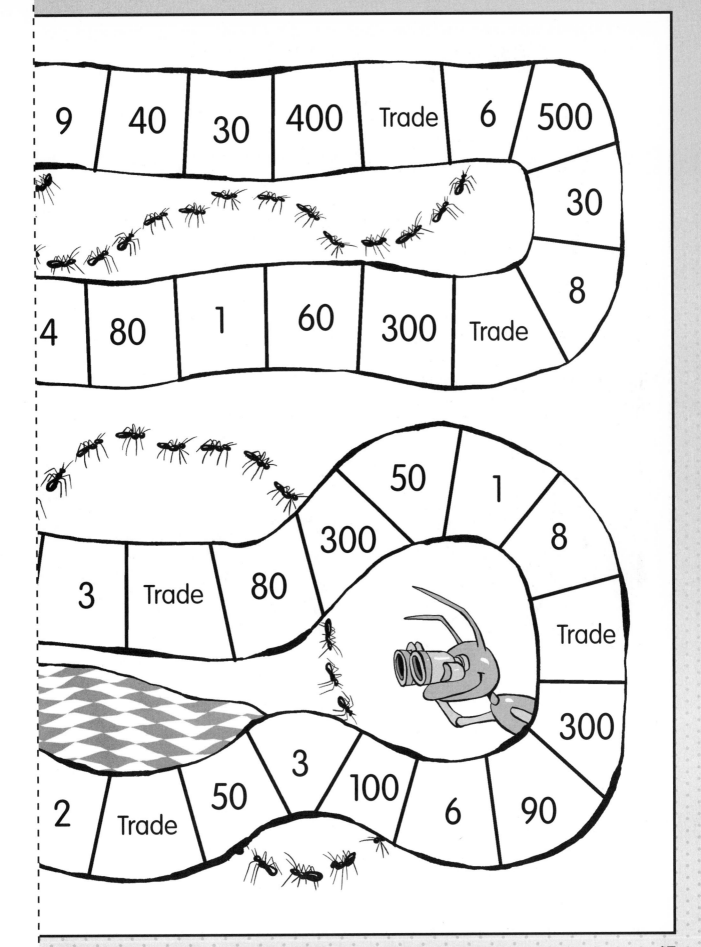

Place Value Picnic	Place Value Picnic	Place Value Picnic
208 Move 1	**657** Move 1	**479** Move 1
Place Value Picnic	Place Value Picnic	Place Value Picnic
190 Move 1	**905** Move 1	**670** Move 1
Place Value Picnic	Place Value Picnic	Place Value Picnic
888 Move 1	**756** Move 1	**301** Move 1
Place Value Picnic	Place Value Picnic	Place Value Picnic
550 Move 1	**283** Move 1	**929** Move 1
Place Value Picnic	Place Value Picnic	Place Value Picnic
466 Move 1	**807** Move 1	**619** Move 1

Place Value Picnic	Place Value Picnic	Place Value Picnic
1,279 Move 2	**8,906** Move 2	**4,050** Move 2
Place Value Picnic	Place Value Picnic	Place Value Picnic
7,008 Move 2	**3,657** Move 2	**6,300** Move 2
Place Value Picnic	Place Value Picnic	Place Value Picnic
2,392 Move 2	**5,501** Move 2	**10,208** Move 2
Place Value Picnic	Place Value Picnic	Place Value Picnic
25,060 Move 2	**46,700** Move 2	**96,524** Move 2
Place Value Picnic	Place Value Picnic	Place Value Picnic
20,007 Move 2	**71,892** Move 2	**99,655** Move 2

Place Value Picnic	Place Value Picnic	Place Value Picnic
249,659 Move 3	**478,770** Move 3	**320,304** Move 3
769,786 Move 3	**606,540** Move 3	**100,567** Move 3
454,706 Move 3	**391,004** Move 3	**1,245,678** Move 3
6,701,409 Move 3	**2,508,250** Move 3	**8,056,110** Move 3
1,253,981 Move 3	**3,598,357** Move 3	**7,032,302** Move 3

Grab It!

Directions:

Manipulatives: plastic spoons (one less than the number of players)

1. Set the plastic spoons in the middle of the table.

2. One player shuffles and deals four cards to each player.

3. The players take turns drawing a card. If the number represented on the card matches a number on a card in their hand, they can grab a plastic spoon. The rest of the players must grab a spoon also. One player will be left without a spoon.

4. The player without a spoon gives one of his or her cards to the player with the match. If that card makes a match, the same player may grab a spoon again. The player with the match lays down each match and reads the numbers to the other players. If there is an incorrect match, the player must give one card to each of the other players.

5. When all the cards in the deck are gone, players may draw a card from any other player.

6. Play continues until all the matches have been made. The player with the most matches is the winner.

Grab It!

2,000 + 900 + 30

Grab It!

2,930

Grab It!

20,000 + 6,000 + 300 + 90 + 9

Grab It!

26,399

Grab It!

4,000 + 200 + 80

Grab It!

4,280

Grab It!

400 + 20 + 8

Grab It!

428

Grab It!

2,000 + 700 + 7

Grab It!

2,707

Grab It!

5,000 + 600 + 8

Grab It!

5,608

Grab It!

60,000 + 4,000 + 500 + 60 + 5

Grab It!

64,565

Grab It!

8,000 + 900 + 60 + 5

Grab It!

8,965

Grab It!

800 + 6

Grab It!

806

Grab It!

80,000 + 7,000 + 500 + 1

Grab It!

87,501

Grab It!

3,000 + 600 + 10 + 2

Grab It!

3,612

Grab It!

30,000 + 5,000 + 200 + 60 + 1

Grab It!

35,261

Grab It!

7,000 + 90 + 6

Grab It!

7,096

Grab It!

900 + 70 + 2

Grab It!

972

Grab It!

10,000 + 6,000 + 400 + 3

Grab It!

16,403

Count the Ants

Directions:

Manipulatives: paper and pencil

1. Each player writes the letters A–F on a sheet of paper. They pass around the ant cards. Each player writes the number of ants by each letter.

2. When the players are finished, they check their answers against the answer card. The player with the most answers correct is the winner.

Answers
A = 124
B = 238
C = 403
D = 267
E = 350
F = 319

Count the Ants
A

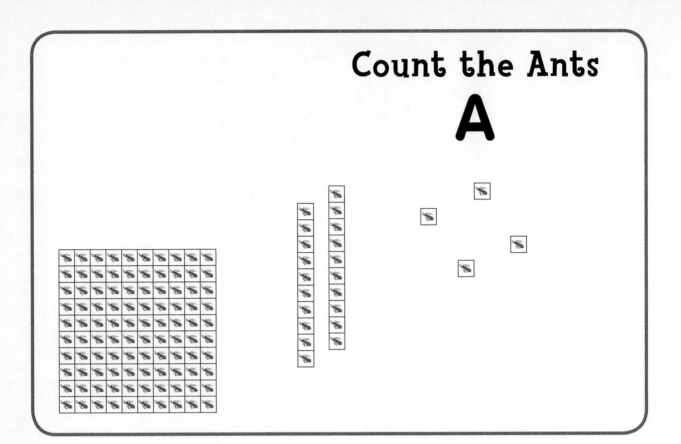

Count the Ants
B

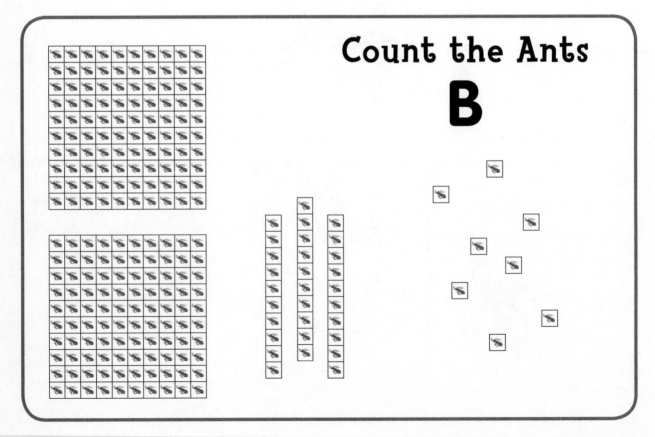

Extra Practice Math Centers: Addition, Subtraction, & More © 2007 by Mary Peterson, Scholastic Teaching Resources

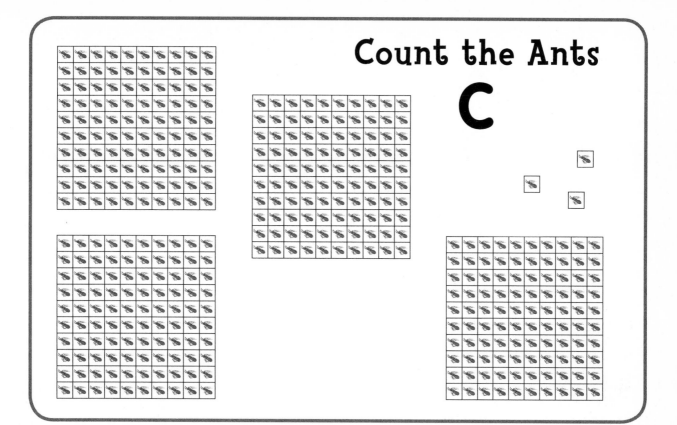

Count the Ants
C

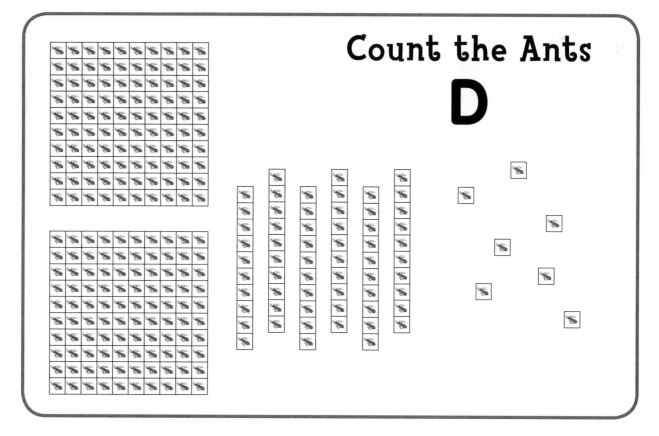

Count the Ants
D

Extra Practice Math Centers: Addition, Subtraction, & More © 2007 by Mary Peterson, Scholastic Teaching Resources

77

Count the Ants
E

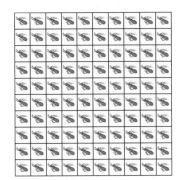

Count the Ants
F

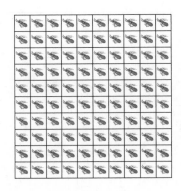
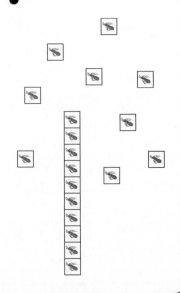

Extra Practice Math Centers: Addition, Subtraction, & More © 2007 by Mary Peterson, Scholastic Teaching Resources

Rounding Sack Race

Directions:

1. Players place their markers on the Start arrow.

2. Players take turns spinning a number and moving their marker that number of spaces along the racetrack. Each player draws a card and rounds the number to the nearest ten, hundred, or thousand depending on the space landed on. Players use the answer card to check their answers.

3. The first player to go around the track *twice* is the winner.

Answer Card

Number	Rounded to 10	Rounded to 100	Rounded to 1,000	Number	Rounded to 10	Rounded to 100	Rounded to 1,000
1,345	1,350	1,300	1,000	22,289	22,290	22,300	22,000
1,763	1,760	1,800	2,000	24,598	24,600	24,600	25,000
1,982	1,980	2,000	2,000	24,675	24,680	24,700	25,000
2,674	2,670	2,700	3,000	24,689	24,690	24,700	25,000
2,745	2,750	2,700	3,000	26,345	26,350	26,300	26,000
3,373	3,370	3,400	3,000	29,831	29,830	29,800	30,000
3,742	3,740	3,700	4,000	31,684	31,680	31,700	32,000
3,819	3,820	3,800	4,000	34,391	34,390	34,400	34,000
4,732	4,730	4,700	5,000	42,693	42,690	42,700	43,000
4,836	4,840	4,800	5,000	45,721	45,720	45,700	46,000
4,854	4,850	4,900	5,000	56,329	56,330	56,300	56,000
5,678	5,680	5,700	6,000	76,354	76,350	76,400	76,000
5,892	5,890	5,900	6,000	86,321	86,320	86,300	86,000
7,852	7,850	7,900	8,000	96,453	96,450	96,500	96,000
8,354	8,350	8,400	8,000	99,678	99,680	99,700	100,000

Rounding

Sack Race

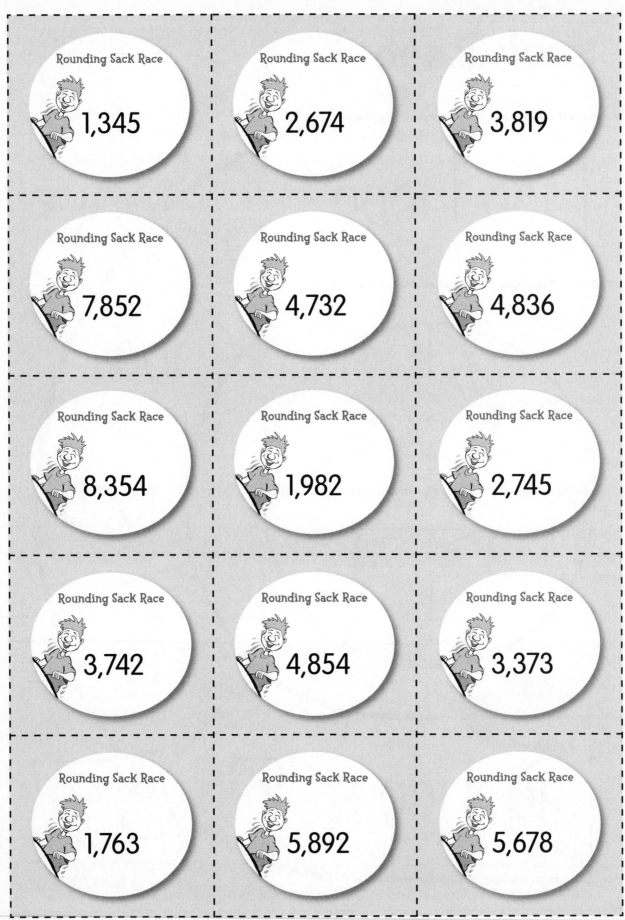

Rounding Sack Race

1,345

Rounding Sack Race

2,674

Rounding Sack Race

3,819

Rounding Sack Race

7,852

Rounding Sack Race

4,732

Rounding Sack Race

4,836

Rounding Sack Race

8,354

Rounding Sack Race

1,982

Rounding Sack Race

2,745

Rounding Sack Race

3,742

Rounding Sack Race

4,854

Rounding Sack Race

3,373

Rounding Sack Race

1,763

Rounding Sack Race

5,892

Rounding Sack Race

5,678

Extra Practice Math Centers: Addition, Subtraction, & More © 2007 by Mary Peterson, Scholastic Teaching Resources

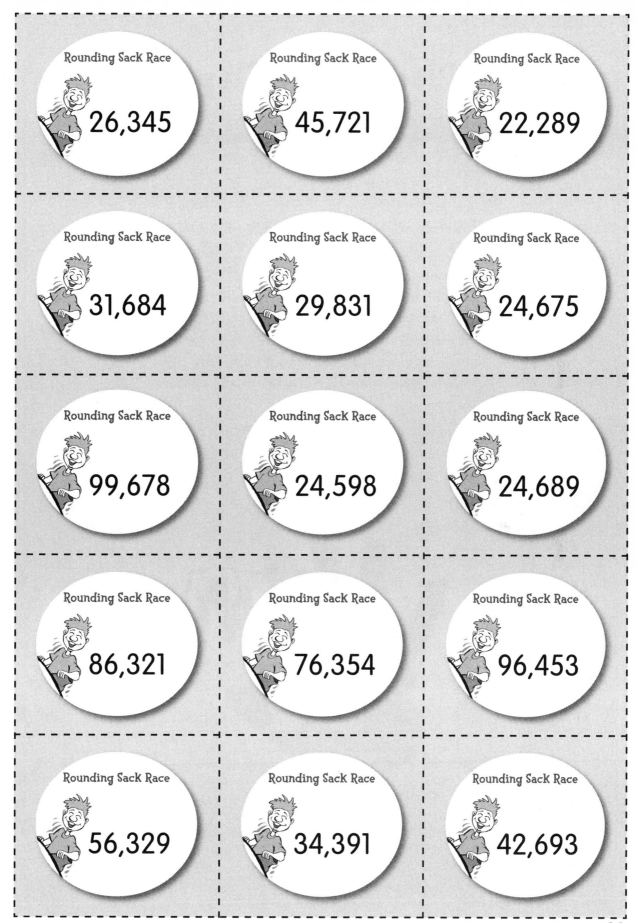

Rounding Sack Race
26,345

Rounding Sack Race
45,721

Rounding Sack Race
22,289

Rounding Sack Race
31,684

Rounding Sack Race
29,831

Rounding Sack Race
24,675

Rounding Sack Race
99,678

Rounding Sack Race
24,598

Rounding Sack Race
24,689

Rounding Sack Race
86,321

Rounding Sack Race
76,354

Rounding Sack Race
96,453

Rounding Sack Race
56,329

Rounding Sack Race
34,391

Rounding Sack Race
42,693

Place Value Slap!

Directions:

1. Shuffle the cards and place facedown in one stack. The first player spins both spinners for a numeral and a place value.

2. A second player turns over one card at a time onto a discard pile. When the number on the card matches the numeral in the place value shown on the spinners, the players slap the card. The first player to slap the card gets to keep the discard pile. If a player slaps incorrectly, all of that player's cards are put back into the stack.

3. When all of the cards are gone from the pile, players each read aloud the numbers on their cards. The player with the most cards is the winner.

Extra Practice Math Centers: Addition, Subtraction, & More © 2007 by Mary Peterson, Scholastic Teaching Resources

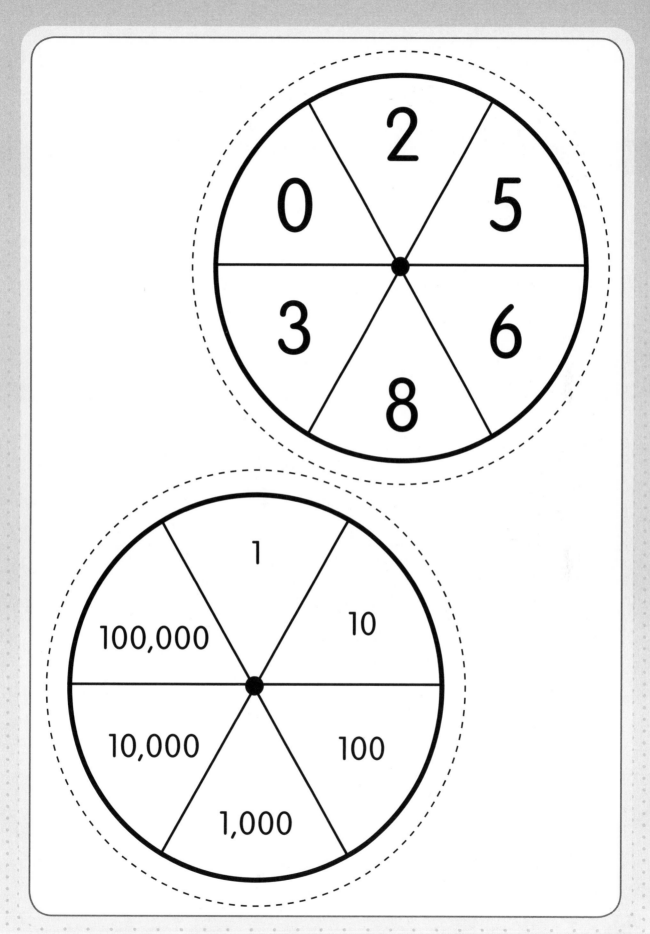

Place Value Slap!

26,538

Place Value Slap!

653,802

Place Value Slap!

328,056

Place Value Slap!

280,563

Place Value Slap!

805,632

Place Value Slap!

56,328

Place Value Slap!

632,805

Place Value Slap!

563,280

Place Value Slap!

526,380

Place Value Slap!

263,805

 Place Value Slap!

638,052

 Place Value Slap!

380,526

 Place Value Slap!

805,263

 Place Value Slap!

52,638

 Place Value Slap!

205,386

 Place Value Slap!

53,862

 Place Value Slap!

538,620

 Place Value Slap!

386,205

 Place Value Slap!

862,053

 Place Value Slap!

620,538

Place Value Slap!

250,683

Place Value Slap!

506,832

Place Value Slap!

68,325

Place Value Slap!

832,506

Place Value Slap!

325,068

Place Value Slap!

683,250

Place Value Slap!

653,802

Place Value Slap!

538,026

Place Value Slap!

380,026

Place Value Slap!

802,653

Extra Practice Math Centers: Addition, Subtraction, & More © 2007 by Mary Peterson, Scholastic Teaching Resources

Number Puzzles

Directions:

1. For each puzzle, make a two-sided copy with the picture puzzle on one side and the number strips on the other side. Cut apart the number strips. (Note: Copy each puzzle onto different colors of card stock.)

2. Players place the number strips in order from least to greatest. After ordering the strips, they turn over all the strips. If the numbers are in the correct order, the puzzle is assembled.

Problem Solving Cards

Directions:

Each student selects a problem-solving card, reads the directions, and solves the problems in a journal.

289

312

394

568

609

976

1,096

1,263

1,540

2,369

1,089

1,980

3,096

5,782

6,002

8,703

10,068

10,098

10,890

12,002

306

312

333

339

346

358

360

381

392

399

405

450

455

4,005

4,050

4,055

4,500

4,550

4,555

5,000

25,895

25,950

30,760

30,906

37,122

37,221

40,009

40,900

49,000

49,009

Burger Town

You have $5.00 to spend on lunch at Burger Town. In your journal, write what you bought, how much it cost, and how much change you received. Write and draw about your lunch.

burger
$1.55

soda
$0.75

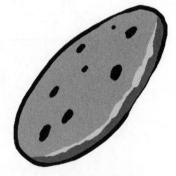

cookie
$0.60

 Extra Practice Math Centers: Addition, Subtraction, & More © 2007 by Mary Peterson, Scholastic Teaching Resources

taco
$1.50

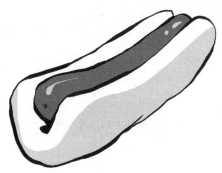

hotdog
$1.25

root beer float
$1.10

fries
$0.55

ice cream
$0.75

Road Trip

It is your vacation. Your trip starts in Hometown. You must choose at least four of the destinations on the map. Your trip ends back at Hometown. In your journal, plan your trip. Figure out how many miles in all you will travel. (The numbers on the map are the mileage between places.) Write and draw about your favorite vacation spot.

 Extra Practice Math Centers: Addition, Subtraction, & More © 2007 by Mary Peterson, Scholastic Teaching Resources

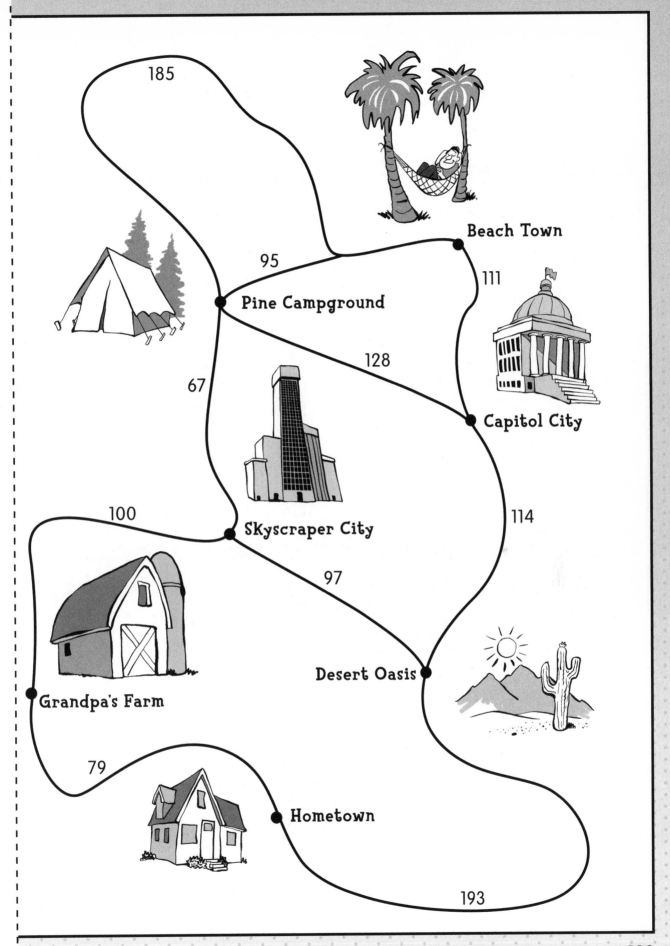

185

Beach Town

95

111

Pine Campground

128

67

Capitol City

Skyscraper City

100

114

97

Grandpa's Farm

Desert Oasis

79

Hometown

193

Bob's
Car Lot

You have $25,000 to spend on a brand-new car from Bob's Car Lot. Choose at least three options for your car. Add the options to the base price of the car to find the total price. Remember, you can't spend more than $25,000.

Figure out how much money you will have left over from the $25,000. In your journal, write and draw a description of the car you are buying. Tell what you will do with the money you have left over.

 Extra Practice Math Centers: Addition, Subtraction, & More © 2007 by Mary Peterson, Scholastic Teaching Resources

Price List

Base Price of Car $20,550
(includes tax and license fees)

Options

CD Player $429

Stereo Speakers $345

Tinted Windows $286

Special Paint Design $856

Cruise Control $594

Leather Seats $1,037

Automatic Windows $653

Special Hubcaps $371

Sunroof $1,294

Keyless Entry $675

Mall

You have $50 to buy at least three items at the Mall Madness Sale. In your journal, record the items you will buy. Figure out the sale price of each item and the total price of the items you are buying. How much money will you have left from the $50? Draw a picture of what you will look like wearing your purchases.

$25.69
Take off $8.99

$25.52
Take off $6.45

$14.99
Take off $6.38

Madness

$28.00
Take off $6.50

$5.55
Take off $1.80

$16.75
Take off $9.00

$35.82
Take off $15.90

$8.85
Take off $2.50

$13.25
Take off $5.80

Measurement Centers

Task Cards

Board Games

Card Games

Puzzles

Measuring Madness Tubs

Directions:

Place each measuring task card and several measuring record sheets in a tub with the manipulatives. Each student follows the directions on the task card and fills in a record sheet. Change the contents of the tub to allow students to measure using standard and nonstandard measuring tools.

Measuring Length

Manipulatives: centimeter or inch rulers, measuring tapes, paper clips, plastic bears, rainbow tiles, coins, items for students to measure, such as different lengths of ribbon, yarn, rope, paper strips, pencils, crayons, and chopsticks

Measuring Area

Manipulatives: rainbow tiles, one-inch ceramic tiles (from home-improvement store), centimeter squares, items for students to measure, such as a washcloth, book cover, tissue, pamphlet, pieces of cloth cut into polygon shapes

Measuring Perimeter

Manipulatives: centimeter or inch rulers, measuring tapes, paper clips, plastic bears, blocks, items for students to measure, such as a washcloth, magazine, place mat, book, newspaper, handkerchief, piece of cloth cut into different shapes

Measuring Volume

Manipulatives: teaspoons, tablespoons, measuring cups, items for students to measure, such as beans, rice, salt, wheat, water, sand, noodles. Provide different-size containers. Label the containers with names or letters for students to identify the container on their record sheets.

Measuring Madness Tubs

Name _____

Measuring _____

Record Sheet		
Item	Estimation	Actual Measurement

Measuring Length

1. Write your name at the top of the Record Sheet.

2. Write the names of the items you will be measuring.

3. Write your estimate of how many _____ long each item will be.

4. Measure each item with the _____ and record the actual measurement.

Measuring Perimeter

1. Write your name at the top of the Record Sheet.

2. Write the names of the items you will be measuring.

3. Write your estimate of how many _____ you could place end to end around the perimeter of each item.

4. Measure the perimeter of each item and record the actual number of _____ you used.

Measuring Area

1. Write your name at the top of the Record Sheet.

2. Write the names of the items you will be measuring.

3. Write your estimate of how many squares you think will cover each item.

4. Find the area of each item by covering it with squares. Record the actual number of square units you used.

Measuring Volume

1. Write your name at the top of the Record Sheet.

2. Write the letter of the container you will be using.

3. Write your estimate of how many _____ of _____ the container will hold.

4. Use the _____ to fill each container with _____ and write the actual number of _____ the container held.

What's My Length?

Directions:

1. Players place their markers on the worm. Shuffle the game cards and set them facedown in a pile.

2. Each player draws a card, reads it, and decides if the item is best measured in inches, feet, or miles. Players move markers to the nearest space that matches their answer.

3. The first player to reach the tape measure wins.

What's My Length?

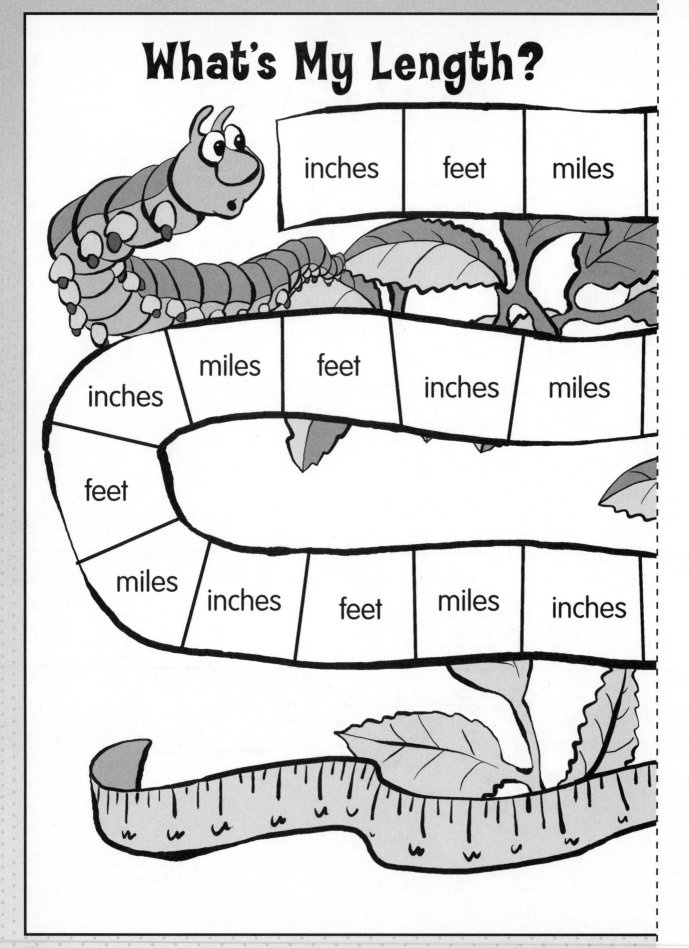

inches | feet | miles

miles | feet | inches | miles

inches

feet

miles | inches | feet | miles | inches

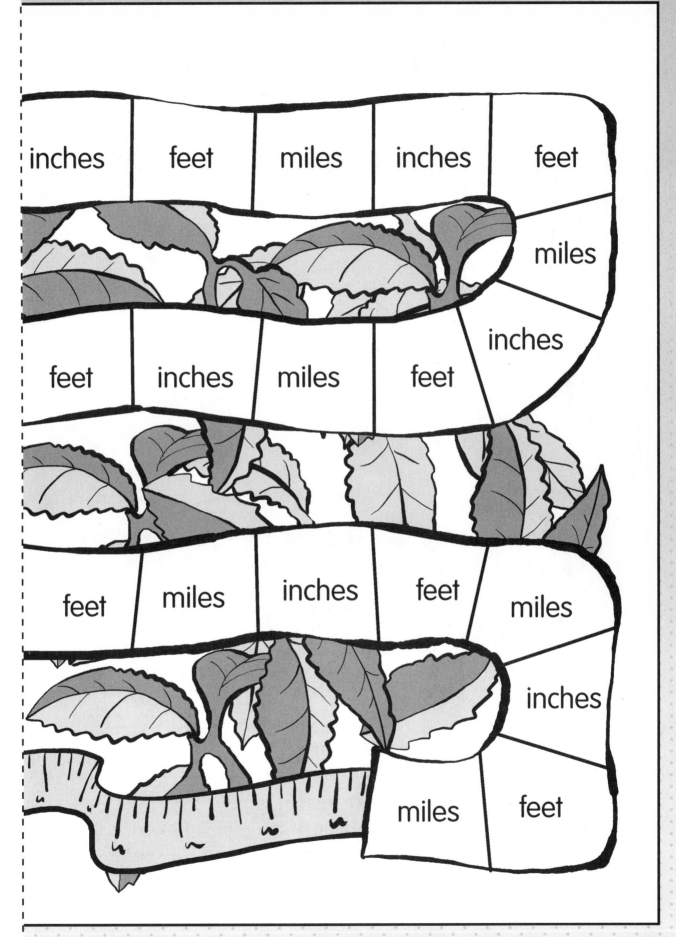

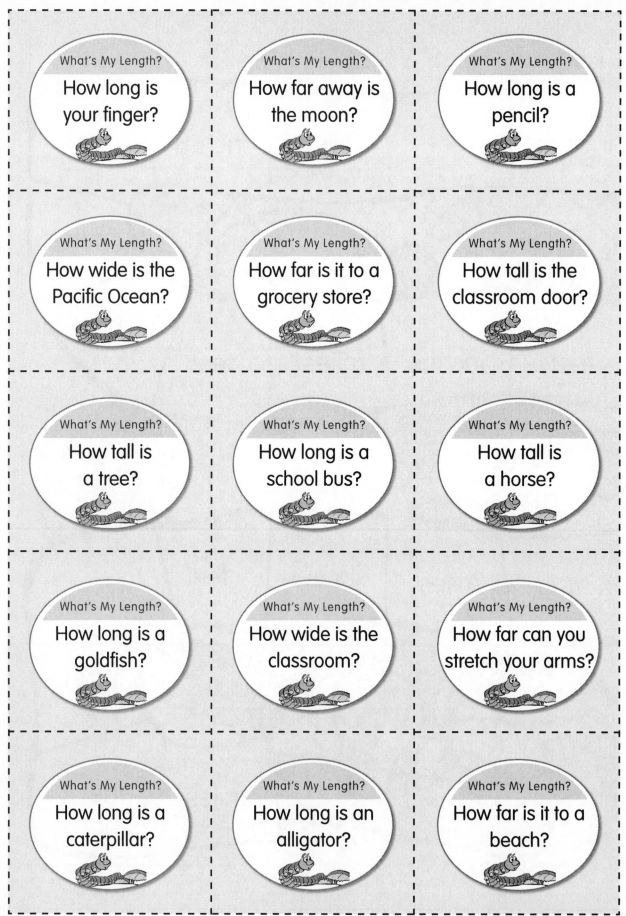

What's My Length?
How long is
your finger?

What's My Length?
How far away is
the moon?

What's My Length?
How long is a
pencil?

What's My Length?
How wide is the
Pacific Ocean?

What's My Length?
How far is it to a
grocery store?

What's My Length?
How tall is the
classroom door?

What's My Length?
How tall is
a tree?

What's My Length?
How long is a
school bus?

What's My Length?
How tall is
a horse?

What's My Length?
How long is a
goldfish?

What's My Length?
How wide is the
classroom?

What's My Length?
How far can you
stretch your arms?

What's My Length?
How long is a
caterpillar?

What's My Length?
How long is an
alligator?

What's My Length?
How far is it to a
beach?

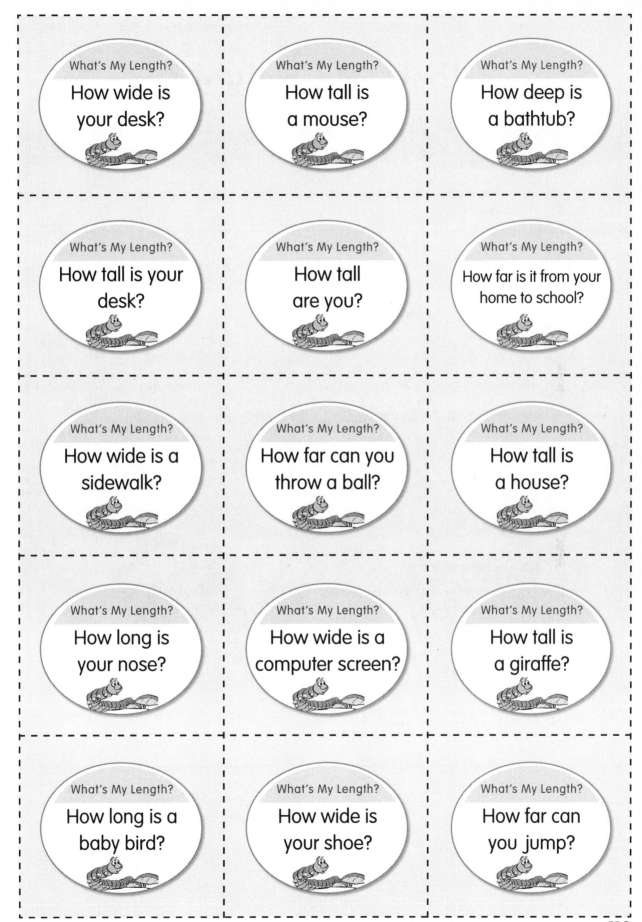

What's My Length?
How wide is your desk?

What's My Length?
How tall is a mouse?

What's My Length?
How deep is a bathtub?

What's My Length?
How tall is your desk?

What's My Length?
How tall are you?

What's My Length?
How far is it from your home to school?

What's My Length?
How wide is a sidewalk?

What's My Length?
How far can you throw a ball?

What's My Length?
How tall is a house?

What's My Length?
How long is your nose?

What's My Length?
How wide is a computer screen?

What's My Length?
How tall is a giraffe?

What's My Length?
How long is a baby bird?

What's My Length?
How wide is your shoe?

What's My Length?
How far can you jump?

What's My Weight?

Directions:

1. Players place their markers on the elephant. Shuffle the game cards and set them facedown in a pile.

2. Each player draws a card, reads it, and decides if the weight of the item is best measured in ounces, pounds, or tons. Players move markers to the nearest space that matches their answer.

3. The first player to reach the scale wins.

 Extra Practice Math Centers: Addition, Subtraction, & More © 2007 by Mary Peterson, Scholastic Teaching Resources

What's My Weight?

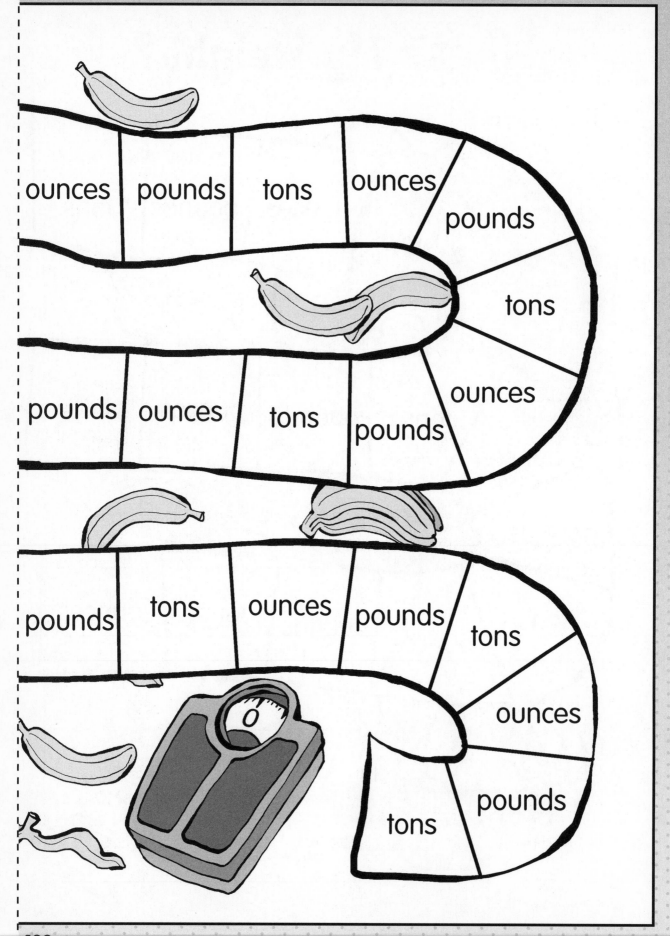

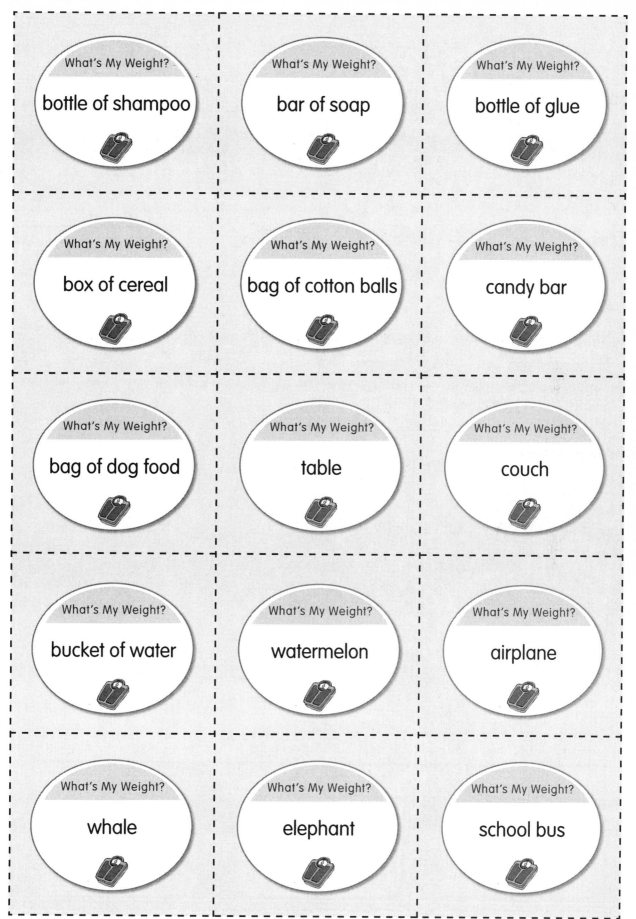

What's My Weight?
bottle of shampoo

What's My Weight?
bar of soap

What's My Weight?
bottle of glue

What's My Weight?
box of cereal

What's My Weight?
bag of cotton balls

What's My Weight?
candy bar

What's My Weight?
bag of dog food

What's My Weight?
table

What's My Weight?
couch

What's My Weight?
bucket of water

What's My Weight?
watermelon

What's My Weight?
airplane

What's My Weight?
whale

What's My Weight?
elephant

What's My Weight?
school bus

What's My Weight?

fire engine

What's My Weight?

van

What's My Weight?

dump truck

What's My Weight?

bottle of water

What's My Weight?

newborn baby

What's My Weight?

glass of juice

What's My Weight?

pair of socks

What's My Weight?

pencil

What's My Weight?

kitten

What's My Weight?

adult

What's My Weight?

turkey

What's My Weight?

pumpkin

What's My Weight?

bag of apples

What's My Weight?

horse

What's My Weight?

box of books

What's My Volume?

Directions:

1. Players place their markers on the measuring cup. Shuffle the game cards and set them facedown in a pile.

2. Each player draws a card, reads it, and decides if the volume of the item is best measured in teaspoons, cups, or gallons. Players move markers to the nearest space that matches their answer.

3. The first player to reach the final square wins.

What's My Volume?

Extra Practice Math Centers: Addition, Subtraction, & More © 2007 by Mary Peterson, Scholastic Teaching Resources

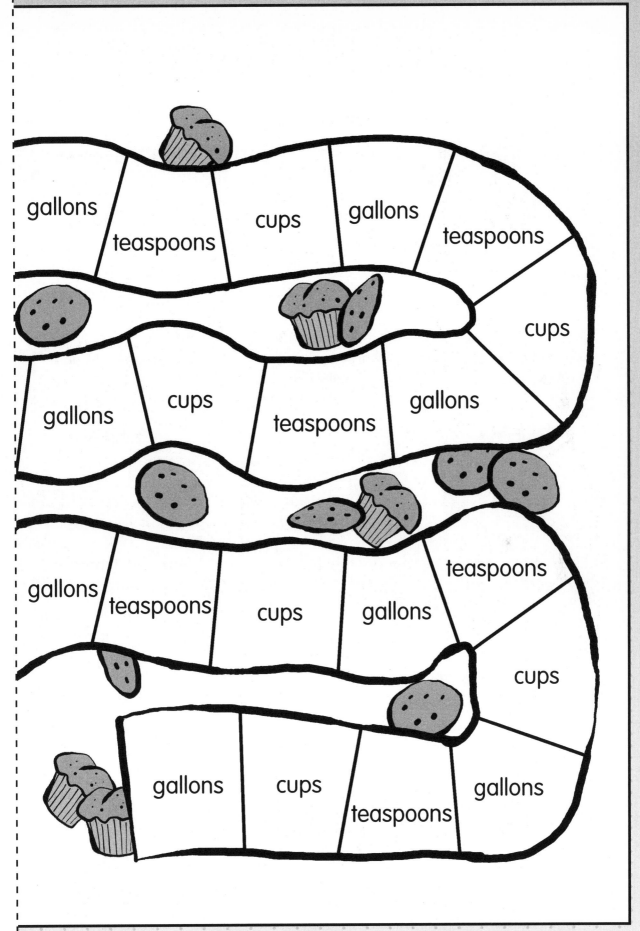

gallons

teaspoons

cups

gallons

teaspoons

cups

gallons

cups

teaspoons

gallons

gallons

teaspoons

cups

gallons

teaspoons

cups

gallons

cups

gallons

teaspoons

What's My Volume?

How much
ice cream is on an
ice-cream cone?

What's My Volume?

How much water
is in a lake?

What's My Volume?

How many
chocolate chips
are in a cookie?

What's My Volume?

How much juice
would the whole
class drink?

What's My Volume?

How much soup
can your whole
family eat?

What's My Volume?

How much syrup
do you put on
a pancake?

What's My Volume?

How much soap
do you use to wash
your hands?

What's My Volume?

How much glue do
you use to stick two
things together?

What's My Volume?

How much mustard
do you put on a
hotdog?

What's My Volume?

How much
dressing do you
put on a salad?

What's My Volume?

How much chili
would feed the
whole town?

What's My Volume?

How much milk
is in a jug?

What's My Volume?	What's My Volume?	What's My Volume?
How much juice is in a glass? 	How much shampoo do you use to wash your hair? 	How much peanut butter is on a sandwich? 
What's My Volume?	What's My Volume?	What's My Volume?
How much water is in a swimming pool? 	How much water fills a bathtub? 	How much milk could the whole school drink? 
What's My Volume?	What's My Volume?	What's My Volume?
How much milk fills a glass? 	How much ketchup do you put on a hamburger? 	How much paint would you need to paint a house? 
What's My Volume?	What's My Volume?	What's My Volume?
How much water would 100 cows drink? 	How much orange juice is in a pitcher? 	How much honey is in a jar? 

Race Around the Clock

Directions:

1. Players place their markers on Start. The first player draws a clock card. He or she reads the time. Another player checks the answer on the answer card. If the answer is correct, the player spins the spinner and moves along the path.

2. The first player to get to Finish is the winner.

Answer Card					
1. 6:00	**7.** 3:30	**13.** 12:15	**19.** 3:45	**25.** 10:05	**31.** 2:50
2. 8:00	**8.** 1:30	**14.** 5:15	**20.** 6:45	**26.** 9:10	**32.** 7:55
3. 9:00	**9.** 4:30	**15.** 8:15	**21.** 5:45	**27.** 8:20	**33.** 9:15
4. 11:00	**10.** 10:30	**16.** 1:15	**22.** 10:45	**28.** 7:25	**34.** 6:30
5. 12:00	**11.** 8:30	**17.** 10:15	**23.** 12:45	**29.** 11:35	**35.** 1:05
6. 2:00	**12.** 12:30	**18.** 7:15	**24.** 8:45	**30.** 4:40	**36.** 4:00

Extra Practice Math Centers: Addition, Subtraction, & More © 2007 by Mary Peterson, Scholastic Teaching Resources

Race Around the Clock

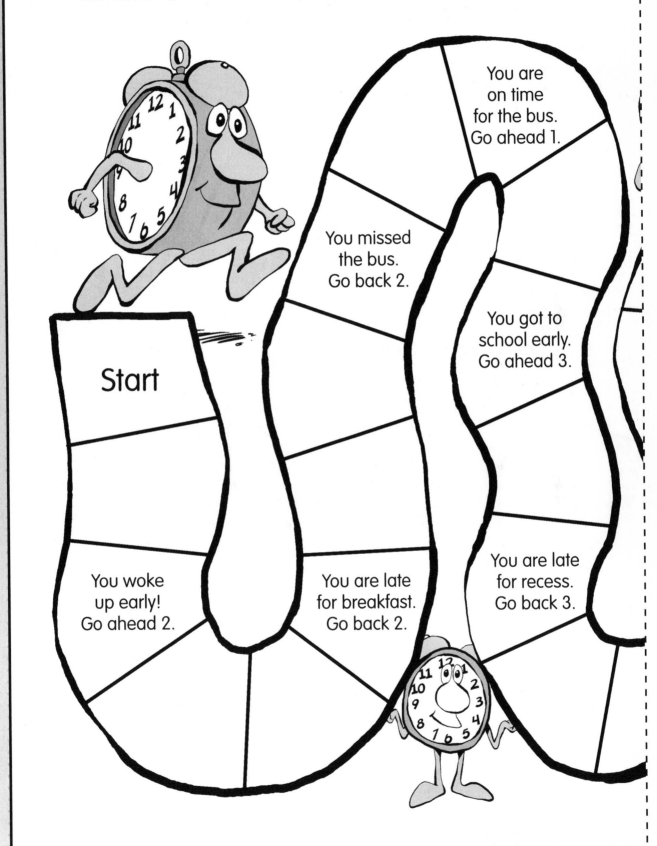

Start

You woke up early! Go ahead 2.

You missed the bus. Go back 2.

You are on time for the bus. Go ahead 1.

You got to school early. Go ahead 3.

You are late for breakfast. Go back 2.

You are late for recess. Go back 3.

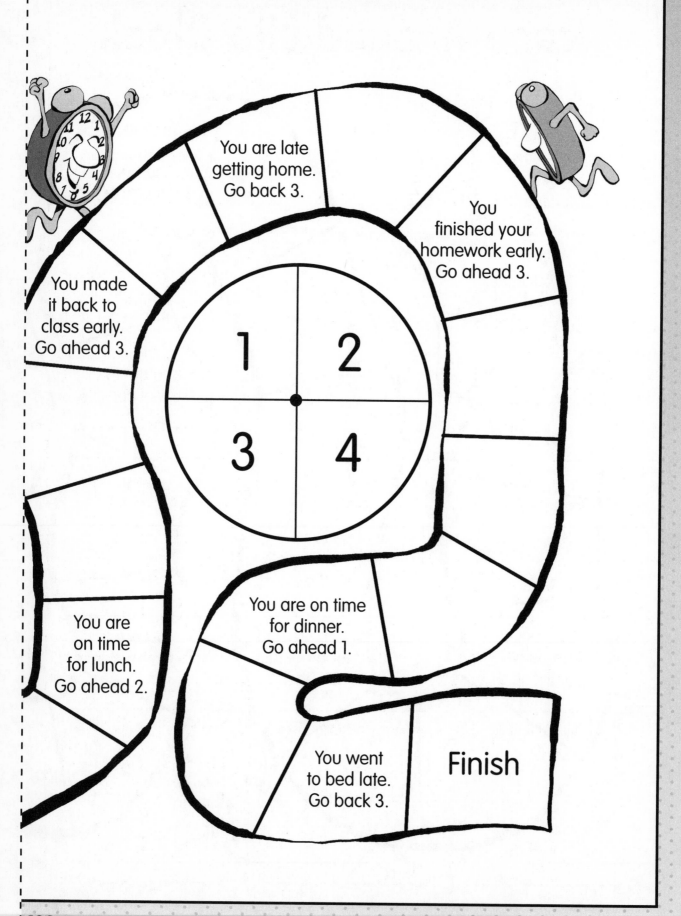

You are late getting home. Go back 3.

You finished your homework early. Go ahead 3.

You made it back to class early. Go ahead 3.

1 2
3 4

You are on time for lunch. Go ahead 2.

You are on time for dinner. Go ahead 1.

You went to bed late. Go back 3.

Finish

Race Around the Clock

Race Around the Clock

Race Around the Clock

13.

14.

15.

Race Around the Clock

Race Around the Clock

Race Around the Clock

16.

17.

18.

Race Around the Clock

Race Around the Clock

Race Around the Clock

19.

20.

21.

Race Around the Clock

Race Around the Clock

Race Around the Clock

22.

23.

24.

Extra Practice Math Centers: Addition, Subtraction, & More © 2007 by Mary Peterson, Scholastic Teaching Resources

Race Around the Clock

25.

Race Around the Clock

26.

Race Around the Clock

27.

Race Around the Clock

28.

Race Around the Clock

29.

Race Around the Clock

30.

Race Around the Clock

31.

Race Around the Clock

32.

Race Around the Clock

33.

Race Around the Clock

34.

Race Around the Clock

35.

Race Around the Clock

36.

How Cold Is It?

Directions:

1. Players place their markers on Start. The first player draws a temperature card. He or she reads the card and decides which temperature is described. Players check the answer on the answer card. If correct, the player spins the spinner and moves along the path.

2. The first player to reach Finish is the winner.

Answer Card		
1. 82° F	**9.** 5° F	**17.** 22° C
2. 95° F	**10.** 120° F	**18.** 0° C
3. 28° F	**11.** 60° F	**19.** 13° C
4. 19° F	**12.** 80° F	**20.** 25° C
5. 73° F	**13.** 28° C	**21.** -16° C
6. 29° F	**14.** 35° C	**22.** 49° C
7. 55° F	**15.** -3° C	**23.** 16° C
8. 75° F	**16.** 1° C	**24.** 27° C

 Extra Practice Math Centers: Addition, Subtraction, & More © 2007 by Mary Peterson, Scholastic Teaching Resources

How Cold Is It?

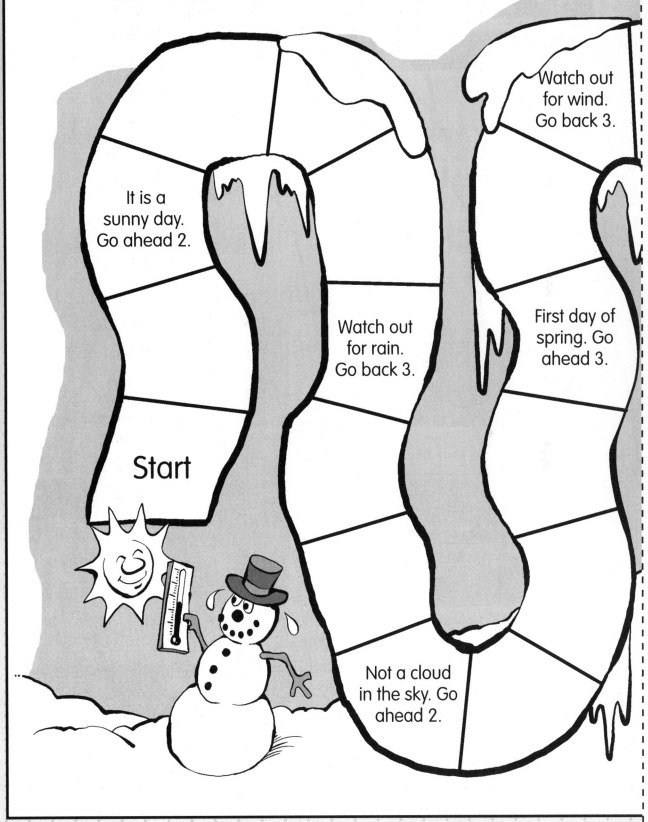

It is a sunny day. Go ahead 2.

Watch out for wind. Go back 3.

Watch out for rain. Go back 3.

First day of spring. Go ahead 3.

Start

Not a cloud in the sky. Go ahead 2.

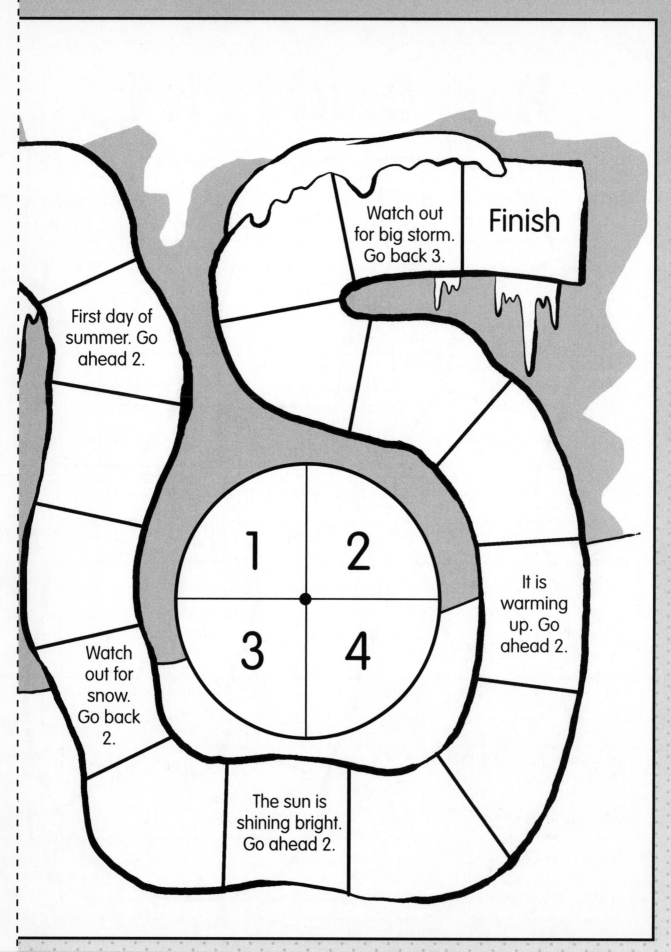

Watch out for big storm. Go back 3.

Finish

First day of summer. Go ahead 2.

1 2
3 4

It is warming up. Go ahead 2.

Watch out for snow. Go back 2.

The sun is shining bright. Go ahead 2.

How Cold Is It?

1.
It's a perfect day
to wear shorts.

23°F 41°F 82°F

How Cold Is It?

2.
It's a perfect day to
go swimming.

32°F 53°F 95°F

How Cold Is It?

3.
It's a perfect day to
make a snowman.

28°F 75°F 100°F

How Cold Is It?

4.
It's a perfect day to wear
mittens, coat, and hat.

19°F 78°F 92°F

How Cold Is It?

5.
It's a perfect day to
play in the park.

-10°F 73°F 115°F

How Cold Is It?

6.
It's a perfect day to
go sledding.

29°F 78°F 95°F

How Cold Is It?

7.
It's a little chilly but not
freezing cold.

30°F 55°F 88°F

How Cold Is It?

8.
It's warm
but not hot.

10°F 75°F 102°F

How Cold Is It?

9.
It's so cold the water in
the pond is frozen.

5°F 45°F 86°F

How Cold Is It?

10.
It's so hot that the
sidewalk burns your feet.

13°F 50°F 120°F

How Cold Is It?

11.
It's a perfect day to wear
a sweater outdoors.

-15°F 60°F 100°F

How Cold Is It?

12.
It's a perfect day to
go to a beach.

0°F 24°F 80°F

How Cold Is It?

13.
It's a perfect day to wear shorts.

....

-6°C 4°C 28°C

How Cold Is It?

14.
It's a perfect day to go swimming.

....

0°C 25°C 35°C

How Cold Is It?

15.
It's a perfect day to make a snowman.

....

-3°C 25°C 38°C

How Cold Is It?

16.
It's a perfect day to wear mittens, coat, and hat.

....

1°C 26°C 34°C

How Cold Is It?

17.
It's a perfect day to play in the park.

....

-20°C 22°C 45°C

How Cold Is It?

18.
It's a perfect day to go sledding.

....

0°C 26°C 38°C

How Cold Is It?

19.
It's a little chilly but not freezing cold.

....

-2°C 13°C 30°C

How Cold Is It?

20.
It's warm but not hot.

....

-12°C 25°C 40°C

How Cold Is It?

21.
It's so cold, the water in the pond is frozen.

....

-16°C 5°C 28°C

How Cold Is It?

22.
It's so hot that the sidewalk burns your feet.

....

-10°C 12°C 49°C

How Cold Is It?

23.
It's a perfect day to wear a sweater outdoors.

....

-25°C 16°C 42°C

How Cold Is It?

24.
It's a perfect day to go to a beach.

....

-18°C 1°C 27°C

More or Less

Directions:

1. Shuffle the cards and place them facedown in a pile. Spin the spinner. (Note: If two players are playing the game, use the More/Less spinner. If more than two players are playing, use the Most/Least spinner.)

2. Each player draws a card and turns it over. Players decide which item weighs more (or most) and which weighs less (or least). If the spinner landed on more (or most), the player whose item weighs more takes all the cards. If the spinner landed on less (or least), the player whose item weighs less takes all the cards. If the items weigh about the same, players draw a second card and play continues.

3. Game continues until all cards are gone from the pile. The player with the most cards wins.

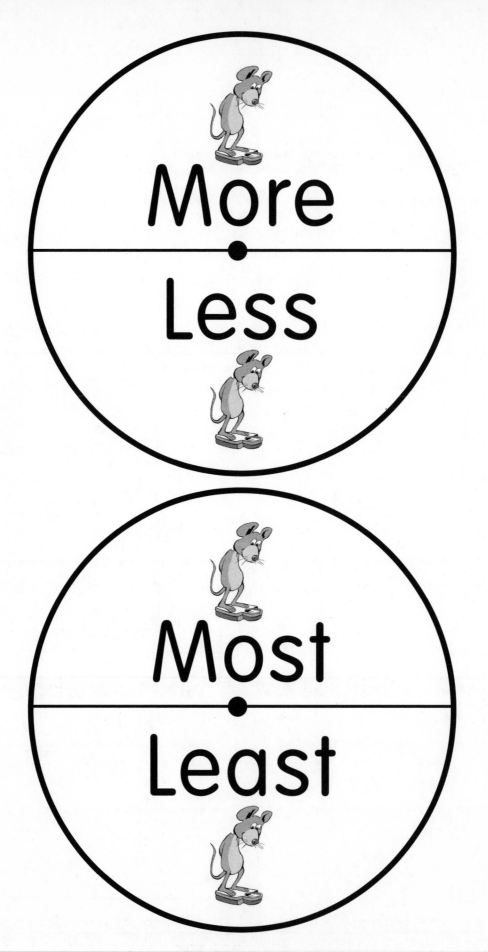

Extra Practice Math Centers: Addition, Subtraction, & More © 2007 by Mary Peterson, Scholastic Teaching Resources

 More or Less

school bus

 More or Less

mitten

 More or Less

shoe

 More or Less

candy bar

 More or Less

lion

 More or Less

baby

 More or Less

bluebird

 More or Less

whale

 More or Less

kitten

 More or Less

apple

More or Less

frog

More or Less

cow

More or Less

pig

More or Less

egg

More or Less

fish

More or Less

snail

More or Less

chicken

More or Less

grizzly bear

More or Less

rhinoceros

More or Less

mouse

 More or Less

rabbit

 More or Less

bicycle

 More or Less

baseball

 More or Less

watermelon

 More or Less

ladybug

 More or Less

pencil

 More or Less

piano

 More or Less

feather

 More or Less

book

 More or Less

elephant

Measuring Around the House

Directions:

1. Players place their markers on the house. Shuffle the game cards and set them facedown in a pile.

2. Each player draws a card, reads it, and decides what the best measuring tool for the task is. Players move markers to the nearest space that matches their answer.

3. The first player to reach the scale wins.

 Extra Practice Math Centers: Addition, Subtraction, & More © 2007 by Mary Peterson, Scholastic Teaching Resources

Measuring Around the House

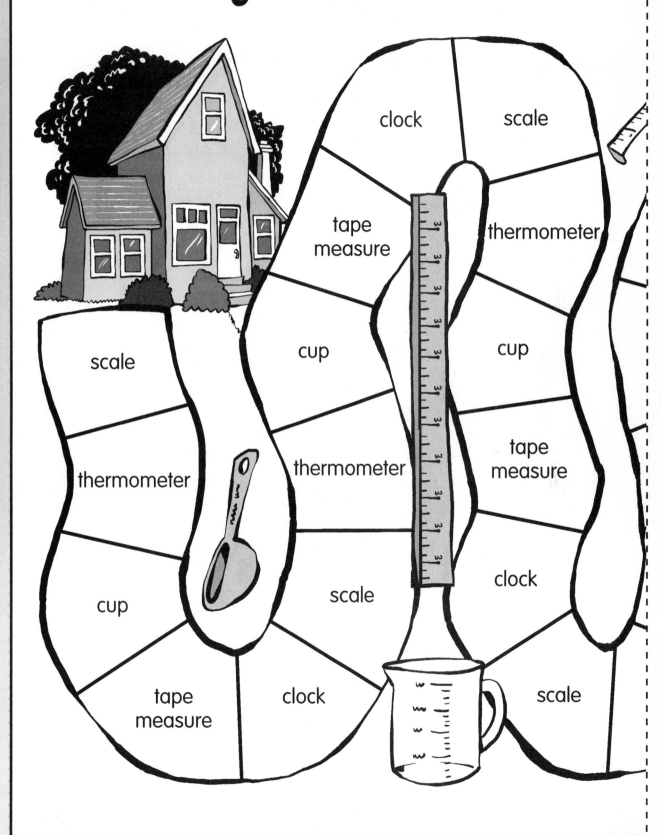

clock

scale

tape measure

thermometer

scale

cup

cup

thermometer

tape measure

thermometer

cup

scale

clock

tape measure

clock

scale

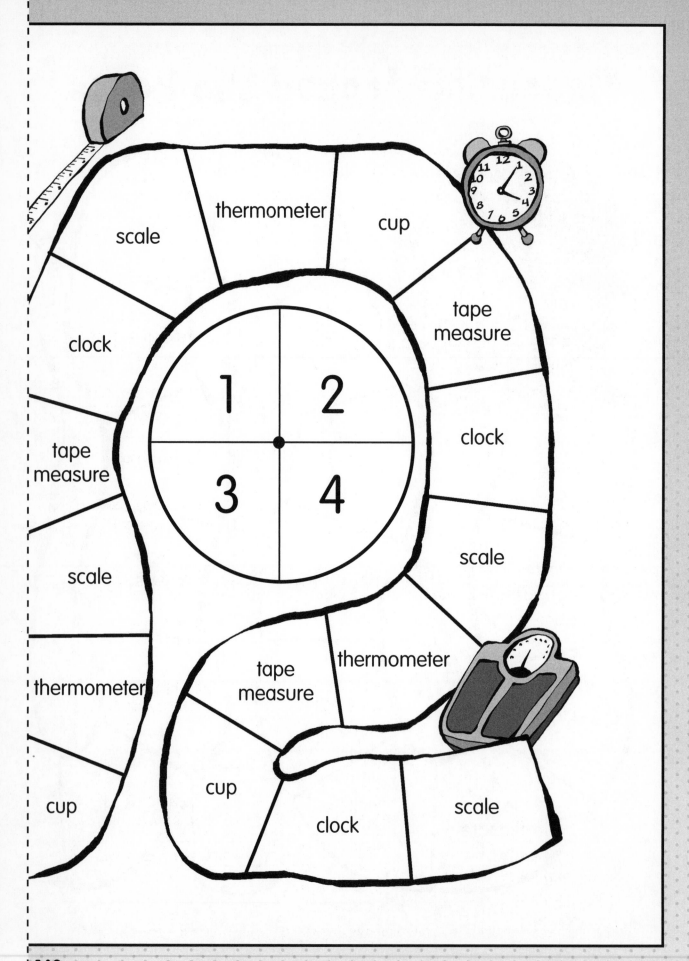

Measuring
Around the House

How much longer
will it be before
dinner?

Measuring
Around the House

I need to read for
30 minutes.

Measuring
Around the House

How much time do
I have before the
bus comes?

Measuring
Around the House

The chicken needs to
bake for 40 minutes.

Measuring
Around the House

Bedtime is in
two hours.

Measuring
Around the House

How long did it
take me to do my
homework?

Measuring
Around the House

Do I need to wear
a jacket today?

Measuring
Around the House

I can't let the
water in the fish tank
get too cold.

Measuring
Around the House

Is it too cold outside
to have a picnic?

Measuring
Around the House

My dad is
checking to see
if I have a fever.

Measuring
Around the House

The turkey is done
when it is 165°F.

Measuring
Around the House

Don't let the house
get colder than 65°F.

Measuring
Around the House

We need an exact
amount of water to
make fruit punch.

Measuring
Around the House

The recipe says
we need an exact
amount of flour to
make biscuits.

Measuring
Around the House

Feed the dog two
cups of dog food.

Measuring
Around the House

Let's make one quart
of hot chocolate.

Measuring
Around the House

The recipe calls for
two cups of milk.

Measuring
Around the House

Give the plant
one cup of water
every week.

Measuring
Around the House

Mom is measuring
the window for
curtains.

Measuring
Around the House

I need to measure
wood to build a
doghouse.

Measuring
Around the House

Dad is measuring
the hallway for
carpet.

Measuring
Around the House

How tall is
the dog?

Measuring
Around the House

How much taller
have I grown?

Measuring
Around the House

Cut a ribbon for
my sister to wear
in her hair.

Measuring
Around the House

Am I heavier than
my brother?

Measuring
Around the House

How much weight
have I lost?

Measuring
Around the House

Does the suitcase
weigh 50 pounds?

Measuring
Around the House

How much does
the dog weigh?

Measuring
Around the House

I can carry seven
pounds in my
backpack.

Measuring
Around the House

A serving of meat
should be four
ounces.

Measurement Puzzles

Directions:

1. For each puzzle, make a two-sided copy with the picture puzzle on one side and the game cards on the other side: pages 153 and 154, 156 and 157, and 159 and 160. Cut apart the game cards. (Note: Copy each puzzle onto different colors of card stock.)

2. Players match the game cards with the information in the boxes on the game board. After all of the cards have been placed, players flips over the cards. If all the answers are correct, the picture will be put together correctly.

Measurement Puzzle 1

60°F

Measurement Puzzle 1

350°F

Measurement Puzzle 1

32°F

Measurement Puzzle 1

-10°F

Measurement Puzzle 1

90°F

Measurement Puzzle 1

212°F

Measurement Puzzle 1

102°F

Measurement Puzzle 1

98.6°F

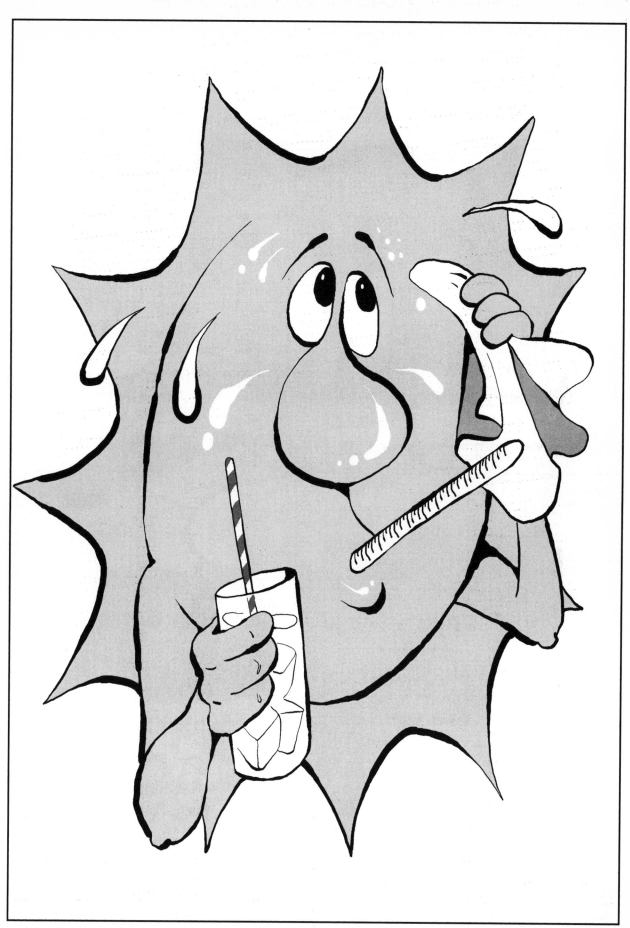

Measurement Puzzle 1

bake a cake

Measurement Puzzle 1

spring weather

Measurement Puzzle 1

too cold to play outdoors

Measurement Puzzle 1

exactly freezing

Measurement Puzzle 1

water is boiling

Measurement Puzzle 1

a hot summer day

Measurement Puzzle 1

normal body temperature

Measurement Puzzle 1

sick with a fever

Measurement Puzzle 2 **cups in a quart**	Measurement Puzzle 2 **inches in a foot**
Measurement Puzzle 2 **pints in a gallon**	Measurement Puzzle 2 **feet in a yard**
Measurement Puzzle 2 **centimeters in a meter**	Measurement Puzzle 2 **pints in a quart**
Measurement Puzzle 2 **pounds in a ton**	Measurement Puzzle 2 **cups in a gallon**
Measurement Puzzle 2 **hours in a day**	Measurement Puzzle 2 **minutes in an hour**

Extra Practice Math Centers: Addition, Subtraction, & More © 2007 by Mary Peterson, Scholastic Teaching Resources

Measurement Puzzle 2 Game Cards

Measurement Puzzle 2

12

Measurement Puzzle 2

4

Measurement Puzzle 2

3

Measurement Puzzle 2

8

Measurement Puzzle 2

2

Measurement Puzzle 2

100

Measurement Puzzle 2

16

Measurement Puzzle 2

2,000

Measurement Puzzle 2

60

Measurement Puzzle 2

24

Measurement Puzzle 3

quarts in a gallon

Measurement Puzzle 3

eggs in a dozen

Measurement Puzzle 3

cups in a quart

Measurement Puzzle 3

days in a week

Measurement Puzzle 3

meters in a kilometer

Measurement Puzzle 3

ounces in a pound

Measurement Puzzle 3

weeks in a year

Measurement Puzzle 3

cups in a pint

Measurement Puzzle 3

inches in a yard

Measurement Puzzle 3

seconds in a minute

Measurement Puzzle 3 Game Cards

Measurement Puzzle 3 **12**	Measurement Puzzle 3 **4**
Measurement Puzzle 3 **7**	Measurement Puzzle 3 **8**
Measurement Puzzle 3 **16**	Measurement Puzzle 3 **1,000**
Measurement Puzzle 3 **2**	Measurement Puzzle 3 **52**
Measurement Puzzle 3 **60**	Measurement Puzzle 3 **36**

Extra Practice Math Centers: Addition, Subtraction, & More © 2007 by Mary Peterson, Scholastic Teaching Resources